UNCONDITIONAL LOVE

Other Superb Books by Dr. Dwayne L. Buckingham

Qualified, yet Single: Why Good Men Remain Single

Can Black Women Achieve Marital Satisfaction? How Childhood Nurturing Experiences Impact Marital Happiness

A Black Woman's Worth: My Queen and Backbone

A Black Man's Worth: Conqueror and Head of Household

Ground-Breaking Films by Dr. Dwayne L. Buckingham

A Black Man's Worth: Conqueror and Head of Household

A Black Woman's Worth: My Queen and Backbone

Qualified, yet Single: Why Good Men Remain Single

www.realhorizonsdlb.com

UNCONDITIONAL LOVE

WHAT EVERY
WOMAN AND *MAN*
DESIRES IN A RELATIONSHIP

Dr. Dwayne L. Buckingham, LCSW, BCD

R<small>HCS</small>

R.E.A.L. Horizons Consulting Service, LLC
Silver Spring, Maryland

Unconditional Love

Unless otherwise indicated, all scripture quotations are taken from the King James Version of the Bible.

To protect the confidentially and privacy of individuals who have shared their stories, identifiable information has been modified.

Additional copies of this book can be purchased on-line at www.realhorizonsdlb.com or by contacting:

R.E.A.L. Horizons Consulting Service, LLC
P.O. Box 2665
Silver Spring, MD 20915
240-242-4087 Voice mail

Expanding Horizons by keeping it "R.E.A.L."

SECOND EDITION

Cover designed by Stephen Fortune

Library of Congress Control Number: 2011962625

ISBN: 978-0-9849423-2-9

Edited by Jennifer R. Jones

For Worldwide Distribution

Printed in the United States of America

Dedication

To every woman and man who desires to give and receive
unconditional love.

Message to Women

Nurture your mind just as much as you nurture your heart. Do not
allow your heart to do what your mind cannot handle. Learn to think,
feel and do. Feeling and doing without thinking is a recipe for
disaster. Love without regret. Do not hold grudges. Experience
unconditional love and change your life. Discontinue the cycle of
pain and bitterness and equip yourself with proper knowledge about
how to love unconditionally; not blindly or foolishly.

Message to Men

Loves starts in the heart, not in the mind. You get what you give. Do
not allow your mind to do what your heart cannot handle. Thinking
and doing without feeling is a recipe for disaster. Love wholeheartedly without straddling the fence and experience unconditional
love that will change your life. Expressing unconditional love for
others enables them to do the same for you. Discontinue the cycle of
fear and equip yourself with proper knowledge about how to love
unconditionally; not apprehensively or fearfully.

My hope is to empower you to love unconditionally as you build and
sustain heartfelt relationships.

I wrote the poem on the next page to inspire you. I hope that you
enjoy your journey as you explore what it means to *Love
Unconditionally.*

Love Unconditionally

I will give you my heart and not fight or flee

But only if you love me unconditionally

Love me for who I am, not who you want me to be

And I will always love you unconditionally

Don't take my love for granted for it's yours to keep

But only if you love me unconditionally

I will love you with all my heart and not resist what is to be

But only if you love me unconditionally

I am not perfect and have character flaws, as you may see

But love me for who I am, not who you want me to be

I have experienced pain and despair as you can see

But will give you my all, if you just love me unconditionally

To earn my love this is the way it has to be

And I apologize that I can't give love like God which is

Unconditionally!

Acknowledgments

First and foremost, I would like to acknowledge my heavenly Father who loves me unconditionally and is the perfect role model for helping me understand how I should love others unconditionally.

Secondly, I would like to acknowledge my beloved and deceased mother, Arlene "Tot" Pettis, who was the first woman to show me what unconditional love means.

Third, I would like to thank my older siblings, Linda, Alma, Cynthia, Bonnie, David and Elisha for being my bedrock and inspiration. They loved me before I knew how to love myself. I would also like to give a special thanks to my younger brother, Dan for being my wingman and best friend as we ventured into manhood.

Fourth, I would like to thank my aunts and uncle Tiny, Louise and Bennie for showing me how to love those who did not love me or themselves.

Fifth, I would like to thank Jennifer Jones for spending numerous hours editing this manuscript and offering her insight. Her contribution was invaluable.

Sixth, I wish to express my appreciation for the work of Albert Ellis, Aaron Beck and Carl Rogers. Ellis and Beck were pioneers in the development of cognitive behavioral therapy (CBT) and Rogers was a humanist who coined the term *Unconditional positive regard*. Unconditional positive regard is blanket acceptance and support of a person regardless of what the person says or does. As a psychotherapist, I use both approaches and have found them to be helpful in assisting couples with resolving personal and relational conflict.

Seventh, I would like to thank the thousands of individuals and couples with whom I have dialogued with in therapeutic, professional and personal settings over the past decade. Without their heartfelt perspectives this book would have less meaning.

Last, but not least, I would like to acknowledge and thank my God sent father, Dr. Richard Chiles for his spiritual guidance, wisdom and unconditional love. Thanks for being the father I never had.

Contents

Contents

**PART THREE: HOW TO SUSTAIN
UNCONDITIONAL LOVE**

**APPENDICES
UNCONDITIONAL LOVE STOPPERS**

What Every Woman and Man Desires in a Relationship

Over the past decade I have spent my professional life as a psychotherapist helping thousands of individuals search for happiness in their relationships. Some individuals seek therapy in an attempt to save relationships that are ending; while others seek therapy in an attempt to enhance relationships that are good, but could be better. Poor communication, disrespect and mistrust are commonly presented as contributors to relationship problems. However, after sorting through the presenting issues, we often discover that the lack of *unconditional love* in the relationship is the underlying problem. Pursuing unconditional love with little or no success is the cause of most failed or troubled relationships.

Whether you are married, engaged, dating or searching for your soul mate, the desire to be loved unconditionally is an underlying motive that ignites most of your thoughts and actions. If you desire unconditional love and believe that it can be achieved, you enter into relationships with honesty and excitement. However, if you desire unconditional love, but do not believe that it is achievable; you enter into relationships with apprehension and uneasiness. The second

-----------------------Unconditional Love-----------------------

1

approach is chosen by most so that they can experience love at some level, but with a guarded heart.

Whether you are married, engaged, dating or searching for your soul mate, the desire to be love unconditionally is an underlying motive that ignites most of your thoughts and actions.

In pursuit of unconditional love, women and men exploit each other emotionally, physically, financially and sexually. This behavior is typically driven by two distinct mind-sets: "conditional love is better than no love at all" or "unconditional love is impossible". Maintaining either mind-set positions individuals to accept whatever they can get or nothing at all; and, the drama that comes with building relationships based on conditional love is only prolonged or delayed.

Like you, I also have experienced the misfortune of being in chaotic relationships and have learned that most people just want to be loved for who they are, not who someone else thinks they are supposed to be. In therapy sessions, women and men regularly ask, "Is it too much to ask others to just love me for who I am. Is this too difficult for people to accept?" I often respond, "Apparently it is". From birth we are taught that love is conditional. How many times have you heard or made one of the following comments:

- Be successful and I will love you even more.

- I love you, but do not upset me or I will leave.

- You do not have to love individuals who do not love you.

- I am not asking you to change, but if you love me you will.

- It is difficult for me to love people who act like that.

- Life is about giving and receiving. If you do not give love, do not expect to receive it.

As loving as most people desire to be, the majority do not understand that the comments they make or the behavior they exhibit daily affects their ability and the ability of others to receive and give unconditional love. The problem for most people is that they have become accustomed to nonsense and look for it in their relationships. As a child I remember my mother telling me to be careful about what I look for because I just might find it. She went on to say that if you look for trouble, trouble will find you. This is so true! I have discovered that most relationships are troubled because people look for trouble and place limits are how they will give love.

Increased feelings of doubt toward self and others cause individuals to reserve their love until they feel certain that they will not be hurt. However, they fail to realize that life offers no guarantees and those who operate in reserve mode: "I will not be hurt ever or again"- do not experience unconditional love or live life to the fullest.

In my career, I have yet to meet a woman or man who does not desire to be loved unconditionally. On the contrary, I have met many who desire unconditional love, but do not know how to receive or give it. Dismayed by this unfortunate occurrence, I began to pay closer attention to the beliefs women and men embrace about relationships. I found that women and men have different views and expectations about relationships, but share one mutual desire— to receive unconditional love. However, the realization of giving and receiving unconditional love seems impossible at times. False images and portrayals of what "attractive or successful" women and men look like continue to penetrate and cloud the minds of millions of good-hearted women and men. Attractive, beautiful and physically fit women and men are idolized. They frequently appear on popular magazine covers, have lead roles in major movies and possess the finer material things in life. Obsession over physical attraction, success, money and fame, has caused many individuals to devalue the "average" woman or man with a good heart.

-----------------------Unconditional Love-----------------------

3

When you think about what you truly desire or have most desired in your current or previous relationship, what comes to mind? What does your checklist of desirable qualities look like? The checklist below is a composite of the top desirable qualities reported by hundreds of individuals with whom I have dialogued with in therapy and social situations.

- ✓ Someone I can get along with
- ✓ Someone I can have fun with
- ✓ Someone who is respectful and trustworthy
- ✓ Someone who is easy to talk with
- ✓ Someone who is sexually compatible with me
- ✓ Someone who is good looking and physically fit
- ✓ Someone who shares similar values, interests and goals
- ✓ Someone who is ambitious and successful
- ✓ Someone who has a good heart
- ✓ Someone who is thoughtful
- ✓ Someone who is spiritual and supportive
- ✓ Someone who is forgiving and patient
- ✓ Someone who is financially stable

Is this list familiar to you? Does it represent qualities that you prefer your mate to possess? Could you love someone who does not possess all or most of the qualities listed above? Could you love someone who possessed them initially, but changed? If you answered yes to both questions, you are destined to have a relationship filled with unconditional love and happiness.

Obsession over physical attraction, success, money and fame, has caused many individuals to devalue the "average" woman or man with a good heart.

After years of struggling to develop relationships built on unconditional love, I decided to examine my list of desirable qualities that I expect my mate to possess and discovered that it resembled the list above. I must say that I was slightly disappointed, but not surprised. After all, I had convinced myself to believe that anyone in their "right" mind would expect their potential mate to have similar qualities. However, after engaging in honest self-reflection it did not take long for me to figure out that the one quality that I truly desired the most was not on my list. Above and beyond all the other qualities, I like most desire to be with someone who will love me unconditionally. Realizing how important this quality is to me, I began to ask myself, why did I exclude it from my list? Was it a conscious or unconscious omission?

As I reflected on my life and the many hardships I have experienced and observed, I concluded at an early age that people cannot love each other unconditionally. This fundamental belief had become entrenched into my emotional reasoning bank. Year after year, I interacted with hundreds of individuals who validated it by displaying conditional love in their relationships. Continually confronted with this reality, I strongly believed that women and men were incapable of loving unconditionally so I decided to place conditions on how I would love others as well. However, as I matured and acquired spiritual knowledge about healthy relation-ships, I realized that unconditional love is possible and that my thinking and behavior was bordering on the edge of insanity. Year in and year out I failed to develop unconditional love in my relation-ships because I believed that I did not have to change how I loved. I continued thinking and behaving the same while expecting that unconditional love would somehow surface in my relationships. I knew my *insane* behavior was not effective, but justified it by telling myself that God knows the condition of my heart. He knows that I "must" have a beautiful wife who possesses all or most of my desirable qualities. I asked myself, "How could I expect anything less if God knows what I desire?" I continued this foolishness for years until I realized that my situation was not changing because the condition of my heart was not right. Let me further explain my dilemma.

Upon meeting women, I immediately placed them in categories prior to even getting to know them. If they were beautiful and physically attractive to me, I put them in the potential mate category. However, if they were average looking and not physically attractive

-----------------------Unconditional Love------------------------

in my opinion, I put them in the friend or see you later category. Sounds shallow right? I agree, now ask yourself how many times you have done the same. The problem with most of us is that our hearts are not centered on what God desires for us, but what we desire for ourselves. My dilemma continued because I persistently justified my insanity by using God's grace as a crutch to judge and categorize women based on conditions. Finally, being the bright and spiritual man that I am, I realized that my thinking and behavior was incorrect because God does not love based on conditions. This simple yet powerful revelation caused me to re-examine my heart and reevaluate my list of desirable qualities. I eventually came to the realization that I could not depend on my emotions to guide me because they changed based on circumstances or conditions. For example, if I "felt" instant chemistry, I opened up; if I did not "feel" instant chemistry, I shut down. I definitely did not understand the meaning of unconditional love. I was on a quick path to being single forever.

I asked God to help me discern the difference between love and unconditional love and He did. Through prayer and fellowship with family and friends, I realized that I was placing too much emphasis on qualities that do not endure when adversity and conflict presents in relationships.

At moments in our lives we might possess some or all of the qualities listed earlier, but it is too difficult to possess all of them all of the time. Over time our minds and bodies deteriorate and the qualities that we believe to be of importance in our youth become less important as we mature. This understanding helped me recognize that the only true quality that will endure when faced with adversity, conflict and aging is *unconditional love*.

Over time our minds and bodies deteriorate and the qualities that we believe to be of importance in our youth become less important as we mature.

The truth is this, no one is perfect. Therefore our qualities change and develop as life throws different challenges our way.

------------------------Unconditional Love------------------------

Sometimes we're at our best and other times we are not. Are you the kind of person who desires to be with someone who is on top of his or her game all the time? If you answered yes, I can relate, but this kind of thinking is irrational and will not allow you to receive or give unconditional love. In fact, it will encourage others to wear their "new shoes" all the time despite the fact that their "old shoes" are more comfortable. What do I mean? Let me explain.

"New shoes" represents what each one of us desires to be or what we believe our potential spouse desires. "Old shoes" represents who we really are. Why do people play the shoe game? Glad you asked! If an individual feels that he or she cannot be him or herself in a relationship, the individual will send a representative who is flawless and wearing "new shoes". However, if an individual feel that he or she can be him or herself, the individual will not send a representative, but will show up with their flaws visible-"old shoes". The "shoe" game can be costly both financially and emotionally because some of us purchase "new" shoes frequently instead of working with or restoring our "old shoes".

Have you ever wondered why so many people change after they are in a relationship? I would argue that most people do not change dramatically, but chose to wear their new shoes until they are comfortable of enough put on their old shoes. Conditional love encourages us to wear the "new shoes" and keep the "old shoes" in the closet until we think the time is right. Past experiences have taught us that it is inappropriate to wear the "old shoes" too soon because we might be judged and thereby miss out on love. This is unfortunate because most people truly and sincerely want to give and receive unconditional love, but engage in this stupidity out of ignorance and fear. Dr. Martin Luther King, Jr. summarized this behavior so gracefully by stating, "Nothing in the world is more dangerous than sincere ignorance and conscientious stupidity". With this in mind, how long will you continue to sabotage your desire to experience unconditional love in your relationship? Will you continue to build relationships based on false hopes and miss out on true love because you refuse to change? What's most important to you?

------------------------Unconditional Love------------------------

7

The only love that endures in any relationship is unconditional love.

Is it important to you to have a relationship that is built on and sustained with love that is conditional and temporary or a relationship that is built on and sustained with love that is unconditional and permanent? No amount of money, success, ambition, compatibility, eagerness or good intention can give meaning to or sustain your relationship like unconditional love can. By now, I hope you get my point: The only love that endures in any relationship is unconditional love.

If you are tired of having bad experiences in your relationships and desire to receive and give unconditional love, this book was written specifically for you. The purpose of *Unconditional Love, What Every Woman and Man Desires in a Relationship* is four-fold: 1) to guide single women and men who desire to develop a relationship built on unconditional love; 2) to inspire married or dating couples to restore or enhance their relationships based on unconditional love; 3) to educate ill-advised women and men about the difference between love and unconditional love; and 4) to give power to the multitudes of women and men who desire to give and receive unconditional love, but do not know how or are afraid.

As you continue to read this profound love guide, remember that any love that is worth having is worth working for. *R.E.A.L.* strategies for developing unconditional love in your relationship are provided to empower you, but your ability to benefit from them will require you to work. Start now by opening up your mind and heart. You deserve to receive everything that God has promised, stop depriving yourself of the one gift that is priceless and can change your life and relationship forever: *your ability to give and receive Unconditional Love.*

PART ONE

UNDERSTANDING LOVE
AND
UNCONDITIONAL LOVE

1

What is Love and Why Does it Hurt?

As I experienced the highs and lows of being in love, I desperately sought answers to two essential questions regarding love's essence and function: What is love? And Why Does It Hurt? Understanding what love is and how it functions is a prerequisite to developing a relationship that is built on unconditional love. Most women and men struggle to understand the real meaning of love. They also struggle to understand how it works. If you do nothing else in your life, please make time to learn about love.

Knowledge of love and how it works provides a road map for developing healthy self-concepts and relationships. *To live life without love is as harsh as living life without a soul.* Given this, I believe that everyone desires love, but they often don't know what it is or how to get it. In talking with others about the meaning of love, I found that a good number of people agree that love is an emotion of compassion. Some individuals report feelings of exhilaration and excitement when they are in love; while others report strong, intense, and indescribable feelings towards another person. Moreover, a widespread consensus is that love should be untainted.

In my quest to understand and help others to understand what love is and how it functions, I created a definition that encompasses both an emotion and action component. I define love as:

A powerful, compassionate and intangible emotion that directs the hearts of women and men.

Before we move on, let's analyze the three terms I used to create my definition of love. *Powerful* is defined as having great force, power or influence; *compassionate* is defined as having feelings of mutual respect, trust, and affection; and *intangible* is defined as hard to pin down or identify. Defining love as I did helped me understand individuals' thoughts and behavior more clearly. These three terms can either set the stage for a relationship from heaven or a relationship from hell.

Some say there is a thin line between love and hate. I never understood what this meant, but I do now. The compassion that enables us to love can also enable us to hate when we hurt. The ones we love the most can hurt us the worst. Why? Because we have allowed ourselves to be vulnerable to them and they know exactly what to do to hurt us. They have the power to influence how we give and receive love, thus the ability to influence our hearts and actions.

We do not mind losing power or control of our hearts if we have compassion for someone. If we believe that they will show us mutual respect, trust and affection, we openly allow ourselves to fall in love; thus giving up the ability to control our hearts. As the emotions intensify and the relationship grows, it becomes more difficult to define how we feel. Love becomes intertwined with other emotions and life events. Initially, feelings of delight and happiness consume us and we truly believe that the feeling of love will never go away.

Most conflict in relationships occurs due to hurt emotions. Especially the one emotion that enables us to feel positive regard and affection toward another: love. As most of us think about love, we associate it with optimistic thinking and positive behavior. Some of us even believe that love conquers all and that relationships can weather any storm if love is present. At one point in my life I believed this; but not anymore. Not to sound too pessimistic, but I have witnessed too many relationships end in which I was convinced that love was present; although many would question whether love was truly present if the relationship ended.

I disagree and this is why. When individuals feel betrayed, wronged, belittled, unappreciated or disrespected, they lash out emotionally and/or physically in order to protect their heart. People have committed murder and other violent acts out of uncontrollable passion or rage. Conflict occurs and is intensified when compassion is lost or minimized due to internal suffering. Love may still be present during or after the conflict, but most individuals are incapable of expressing it in a compassionate manner when they are hurting.

People have a difficult time coping with being hurt because they believe that love should not hurt. Unfortunately, this flawed thinking causes many to walk away from their relationship or marriage because they are hurt. You are probably thinking that if love is supposed to be positive and optimistic, it should not hurt.

Adjust your thinking....Love Does Hurt, But not intentionally!

Let me explain why I believe that love hurts! Love hurts because human beings are imperfect. We hurt each other sometimes consciously and sometimes unconsciously. How many times have you heard individuals say, "I love you and did not intend to hurt you"? I defined love as a powerful, compassionate and intangible emotion that directs the heart of women and men. This means that the heart is the control center that manages the emotions that influence our love. In reality, our hearts and emotions, like other things in our lives, change with conditions and circumstances. We withdraw or limit our love when our emotions are hurt and more often than not, we end up hurting ourselves and others in the process. Although we do not like the pain that is associated with withdrawing or limiting our love, we do so to protect our hearts. The bottom line is that love hurts because we are imperfect and we often engage in self-preserving behavior in order to protect our hearts.

You must realize that love in and of itself is not enough to prevent us from hurting each other. Human beings were created out of love to love, but we allow our emotions to distort that love. I suggest that you look at the intent of a person's heart before you eliminate him or her from your life completely. I have learned that good hearted people say and do bad things when their feelings are hurt. As a result, I try to pay close attention to their underlying motives. If I detect that they are hurting me because they lack insight as to how to express their emotions appropriately; I provide support, guidance and prayer. Basically, I stick with them. If I detect that they are deliberately hurting me to be spiteful; I also provide support, guidance and prayer. If the deliberate behavior continues, I simply remove myself from the situation. Adjust your thinking one more time; love does hurt, but not intentionally!

Without question, the essence and function of love is debatable. Due to individual and cultural differences, it is too difficult, if not impossible, to obtain a universal agreement on what love is and how it functions. However, most people would agree that the meaning and application of love can be best clarified by exploring what it is not:

- Love is not hate
- Love is not resentful
- Love is not conditional
- Love is not pride

- Love is not limited
- Love is not a gift from man
- Love is not to be taken for granted
- Love is not restricted to a specific race or gender
- Love is not abuse
- *Love is not lust*
- Love is not physical, but can be expressed through physical means
- Love is not forced, it is a choice

It is important to understand what love is and is not. Those who fail to learn about love position themselves to be deprived of experiencing true love and often search for love in all the wrong places and from the wrong people. Comprehending the essence and function of love can help you determine if you should enter or remain in a relationship, as well as help you determine if your relationship is built on and sustained on a solid foundation.

Love is not Lust

Relationships that are based on love are more likely to last as compared to relationships that are developed out of a strong physical attraction or lust. An issue that continues to astonish me daily is the belief that individuals are capable of falling in love at first sight. I am not sure that this is possible. I do believe that individuals are capable of falling in lust at first sight. Why do I say this? Love is associated with internal attributes (personality, values, the condition of a person's heart, etc.) and lust is associated with physical attributes (nice face, nice butt, sex appeal, etc.). Love requires you to be in a person's presence in order to develop feelings. Lust requires nothing more than a lustful eye. Love develops emotional intimacy while lust develops physical intimacy that is often mistaken for emotional intimacy. Many individuals build relationships out of lust because they do not understand what real love is. Have you ever listened to a person describe his or her current or potential spouse?

How much emphasis is placed on the physical attributes as compared to the internal attributes?

Love is not Lust...*there is a difference!*

Women and men have confused Love with Lust without realizing that they operate in opposition to each other:

L Love makes you wait to be married before having sex

£ Lust makes you jump in the bed before marriage

L Love enables you to appreciate your significant other's mind

£ Lust enables you appreciate your significant other's body

L Love makes you yearn for your significant other

£ Lust makes you yearn for someone else's significant other

L Love makes you turn to God and your significant other when trouble is present in your relationship

£ Lust makes you turn away from God and your significant other when trouble is present in your relationship

L Love makes you come home and hold your significant other

£ Lusts makes you stay away from home and hold someone else's significant other

L Love contributes to faithfulness

£ Lust contributes to infidelity

L Love enables you to validate, respect and honor your significant other's emotions

£ Lust contributes to invalidation, disrespect and dishonor

I cannot stress the importance of understanding what love is and how it functions. One cannot remove lust or any other vice from his or her life unless he or she understands what love is. We are living in times when more emphasis is placed on physical qualities and less on internal qualities. This trend is especially dangerous for women and men who define their worth and their spouse's worth by their physical and sexual qualities.

I want to clarify the difference between love and lust because relationships built on love enable individuals to give and receive love. Relationships built on lust cripple individuals and limit their ability to give and receive love. Love does not fade when physical attributes falter, but lust does. Love can repair lust, but lust cannot repair love. Love lasts as long as emotional attraction is strong. Lust lasts as long as physical attraction is strong. What is your relationship built on?

Love = mutual respect, trust and affection: Strong Emotional Intimacy

---

Lust = one sided or mutual disrespect, mistrust and detachment: Strong Physical Intimacy

Embrace love and receive all that you can from it, but do not live your life believing that love does not hurt or confusing it with lust! Remember that love is a gift from God. It is a powerful, compassionate and intangible emotion that directs the hearts of women and men. For this reason, love is not to be played with for it can destroy hearts. Now that you have acquired an understanding of what love is you are one step closer to being able to give and receive the unconditional love that you desire in your relationship. One must

-----------------------Unconditional Love-----------------------

first understand what love is before he or she can comprehend the depth and meaning of unconditional love. In the next chapter we will explore what unconditional love is and how it functions.

"Love is what you make it; so make the best of it"

What does love mean to you?
What is your relationship built on?
Why do you choose to love or not too love?
Should or does love hurt? Why or Why not?

_____
_____
_____
_____
_____
_____
_____
_____
_____
_____
_____
_____
_____
_____
_____
_____
_____
_____
_____
_____

----------------------Unconditional Love----------------------

2

What is Unconditional Love?

L ike love, the essence and function of unconditional love is debatable and is too difficult, if not impossible, to obtain a universal agreement on what it is and how it functions. Secular and spiritual counselors have similar thoughts about what unconditional love is and how it functions. Secular counselors refer to unconditional love as being true love between two individuals who love each other regardless of each others' actions or beliefs. Spiritual counselors use the same characterization but also include forgiveness.

It is my belief that the spiritual definition of unconditional love is most appropriate for individuals who desire to develop relationships that last forever. True forgiveness is required for sincere reconciliation. Many people do not think that unconditional love is possible, but that is because they do not associate it with a Higher Power. Unconditional love is not just about acceptance, also has a forgiving and nonjudgmental component. God not only accepts us as we are with our imperfections and all; He also forgives us and allows us to redeem ourselves after we engage in inappropriate behavior. He does not withdraw or limit His love. This is the basis of unconditional love. Let me summarize what I believe unconditional love is:

A powerful, compassionate and intangible emotion that directs the hearts of women and men with forgiveness and positive regard.

A thorough comprehension of unconditional love and how it works enables individuals to love others irrespective of the other person's love for them. You can give and receive unconditional love if you learn to address unacceptable behavior without attacking character flaws by withdrawing or limiting your love. As captured in my definition, unconditional love means to forgive and demonstrate positive regard for others.

Forgiveness requires you to remove resentment and anger from your heart in order to develop positive regard for others. Positive regard is a term that was coined by Carl Rogers, a humanistic psychologist who believed that all people have internal resources that are needed to grow. Demonstrating positive regard towards another will enable them to facilitate personal change. Positive regard involves acceptance of an individuals' behaviors and words without judging them. In listening with a non-judgmental attitude you can potentially help individuals see and accept responsibility for their actions. You simply facilitate change, not force it. This is important because most people feel that internal change is more gratifying than external change and typically lasts longer. Be mindful that we all get annoyed with each other, but by demon-strating positive regard we can nurture healthy personal growth. No one likes to be reminded of his or her shortcomings in a negative, judgmental or insensitive manner.

It is imperative that you comprehend what it means to love unconditionally. Your ability to weather storms in your relationship is greatly influenced by your comprehension of unconditional love. Relationships evolve and thrive when individuals love each other unconditionally and understand that their initial attraction is simply a building block, and is not the key to sustaining their relationship.

So often individuals rely on love to get through tough times and I would argue that they are relying on the wrong source. Love is a good a place to start, but adversity in relationships is conquered with unconditional love. Love is not unconditional love. There is a difference.

---

*Love is not **Unconditional Love...** there is a difference!*

Most people accept love, but truly desire unconditional love. Love is temporary. Why? Relationships are usually built from love that meets individuals' emotional and physical needs in the interim. As individuals grow in a relationship, they often find that initial love fades. As that initial love fades, the relationship weakens and unconditional love is desired more intensely. While it is true that one cannot achieve unconditional love in their relationship without having some level of love, love does not have the same impact on relationships as unconditional love does. Here's how love and unconditional love differ:

Ł   Love builds relationships

ÚŁ   Unconditional love sustains them

Ł   Love enables you to remain in a relationship with resentment and anger in your heart

ÚŁ   Unconditional love enables you to remove resentment and anger from your heart

Ł   Love makes you come home

ÚŁ   Unconditional love makes you enjoy being at home

Ł   Love feels good most of the time

ÚŁ   Unconditional love does not always feel good, but is good for you and those you love

Ł   Love is easy to develop and requires little work; a good heart with good intentions

ÚŁ   Unconditional love is difficult to develop and requires work; a forgiving heart with positive regard for others

Ł   Love is emotionally driven

ÚŁ   Unconditional love is spiritually driven

Ł   Love evolves through physical proximity, similarities and physical attraction

ÚŁ   Unconditional love evolves through a relationship with God

The most distinguishing characteristic of unconditional love is that it never fails. Loving unconditionally empowers individuals to accept the bad with the good and remain committed to maintaining joyful and healthy relationships. Unconditional love moves individuals to support each other, work together, and communicate openly with one another.

Unconditional love sees no limits, feels no limits and accepts no limits.

Your heart can be conditioned to do whatever you want it to do. Why not condition it to love others unconditionally? Unconditional love sees no limits, feels no limits and accepts no limits. If you believe in unconditional love and work to develop it in your relationship, you will reap the benefits of giving and receiving like never before. Sounds simple right? Well it is not. Loving unconditionally is not as easy for some people as it is for others. Why? Just as individuals learn how to walk, talk and eat, they also learn how to love. Understanding why and how you love is critical and will affect how you experience and view relationships from this point on. In the next chapter, *Discover Your Love Style*, I identify the different love styles, explain how they develop and clarify why some people are capable of giving and receiving unconditional love easier than others.

"Women and men who delight in unconditional love,
delight in the fullness of life"

What does unconditional love mean to you?
Do you believe it is possible to give and receive
unconditional love? Why or Why not?

_____
_____
_____
_____
_____
_____
_____
_____
_____
_____
_____
_____
_____
_____
_____
_____
_____
_____
_____
_____
_____
_____

--------------------What is Unconditional Love?--------------------

3

Discover Your Love Style

Are you a Conditional Lover or an Unconditional Lover?

U nderstanding your love style is a challenging yet essential task. Knowing how you love will help you cope effectively when faced with adversity in your relationship. Conflict arises in most relationships when one or both individuals feel that they are not being loved unconditionally. The conflict worsens if one or both individuals continually fail to love their significant other in a manner in which he or she desires to be loved. Why does this happen? Excellent question! Unfortunately, many individuals do not understand their own love style. As a result, they struggle to effectively respond to the needs of their significant other as well as their own needs. Lack of knowledge regarding how to love self and others unconditionally is linked to an individual's lack of knowledge about their love style. In order to build a relationship based on unconditional love, you must first understand the two love styles, be able to distinguish one from the other and be aware of how your love style developed. Please allow me to enlighten you.

Conditional Lovers

Conditional lovers give and receive love based on conditions that must be met. This love style is frequently used out of a desire to control one's self or others by limiting or restricting love. Individuals who deploy this love style have a strong need to be in control. Being in control empowers them to master their destiny and minimizes their risk of being vulnerable. Without displaying vulnerability, they avoid the risk of being hurt and also prevent themselves from giving or receiving unconditional love. Conditional lovers are motivated by receiving and giving, but the fear of pain, suffering and disappointment intensifies their need to receive before giving. An exchange is frequently required. Here are a few examples:

- You respect me and I'll respect you

- You love me unconditionally and I will love you unconditionally

- You talk to meet respectfully and I will talk to you respectfully

- You trust me and I will trust you

- You forgive me and I will forgive you

Conditional lovers usually search for and settle down with individuals who have high market value. Physical appearance, wealth, behavior, religious convictions, emotional and intellectual status are used by conditional lovers to determine if, how much and when to give love. Willingness to love unconditionally is strongly influenced by external factors instead of the condition of a person's heart. Individuals who love conditionally often strive to control others: "If I just give my all, he or she will change; if I enforce my will on him or her I will get what I want". If conditional lovers are not capable of controlling others, they turn their energy inwardly and focus on self. They become high achievers who focus on things they can control and minimize their emotional need to be with others, especially individuals they cannot control. This profound need to control one's self and others contributes to feelings of inadequacy, hopelessness, loneliness, helplessness, sadness, anger, greed, bitterness, fear and even hatred if efforts to gain control are unsuccessful. Generally speaking, conditional lovers are inpatient and will try to force or control relationship outcomes instead of allowing them to evolve naturally. Engaging in a relationship is viewed as a process to be controlled, not experienced. They plant the love seed and then attempt to control how it grows.

Conditional lovers typically practice selfishness, rigidity, and use "I talk": I want, I must have and I need. "I talk" is common among conditional lovers. Also be aware that conditional lovers frequently withhold or limit their love based on "standards". Standards are synonymous with conditions. Is this your love style?

Engaging is a relationship is viewed as a process to be controlled, not experienced. They plant the love seed and then attempt to control how it grows.

Side note: If you are a conditional lover, please stick to your conditions or standards. I say this because it is not fair to you or your significant other if you lower your standards. People who believe that they have "settled" are typically not happy and will always have a yearning for what they think they are missing. If you like a woman or man with a certain build, look or intellect you should date individuals who meet your criteria. Be careful when dating people who do not meet your criteria...love will and can creep up on you and before you know it you are in a relationship and unhappy. However, if you end up in a relationship with someone who does not meet all of your standards, learn to love him or her unconditionally.

Unconditional Lovers

Unconditional lovers give and receive love regardless of conditions, even when the return is insufficient or non-reciprocal. What does this mean? We all want something in return right? Yes, but unconditional lovers do not withdraw or restrict their love if the return is insufficient. This love style is most frequently used by individuals who desire to influence others by allowing them to be themselves. Individuals who practice this love style rejoice in giving love just as equally as they rejoice in receiving it.

Unconditional lovers allow others to exercise their *free will* because they realize they cannot control others. Additionally, unconditional lovers search for the essence of a person's character and place emphasis on the condition of the person's heart; not their outwardly appearance, achievements or status. Like conditional lovers, unconditionally lovers also desire to be with an attractive, smart and financially stable individual. However, they are more inclined to allow themselves to fall in love with an individual who has an amazing soul. Unconditional lovers are aware that loving unconditionally makes them vulnerable and can potentially cause suffering; but they are also aware that they cannot experience unconditional love unless they allow themselves to be vulnerable. An exchange is not required, but is greatly appreciated. Here are a few examples:

- I respect you and prefer that you respect me

- I love you unconditionally and I hope that you love me the same

- I talk to you respectfully and would appreciate the same consideration

- I trust you, but it is up to you to trust me

- I forgive you and you can chose to forgive me

Unconditional lovers typically search for and settle down with individuals who have average market value, but high market potential. The desire to influence others empowers unconditional lovers to control the things they can control and let go of the things they cannot. This profound understanding of influence contributes to feelings of peace, happiness, calmness, respect, trust, compassion and appreciation which are manifestations of loving unconditionally. Usually, unconditional lovers are patient. They allow relationship outcomes to evolve naturally instead of trying to force or control them. Engaging in a relationship is viewed as a process to be experienced, not controlled. They plant the love seed and allow it to grow without attempting to control it.

Unconditional lovers typically practice selflessness and use "we talk": We want, we must have and we need. "We talk" is common among unconditional lovers. Is this your love style?

Engaging in a relationship is viewed as a process to be experienced, not controlled. They plant the love seed and allow it grow without attempting to control it.

Major Distinction between Conditional and Unconditional Lovers

The major distinction between the two love styles is centered on the intent. Conditional lovers intend to control others' behavior and unconditional lovers intend to influence others' behavior. Conditional lovers attempt to prevent or limit individuals from exercising their *free will* by withdrawing or restricting their love. In contrast, unconditional lovers allow individuals to be themselves without withdrawing or restricting their love. The ability to forgive and show positive regard for others separates unconditional lovers from conditional lovers. Which love style do you prefer?

-----------------------Unconditional Love-----------------------

33

IDENTIFYING LOVE STYLES KNOWLEDGE QUIZ

Let's see if you can identify the different styles of love. Circle the correct answer for each question. The answers are listed at the end of the quiz. Good luck.

1. "I only give love if I receive it. Life is too short to give and not receive. If I am angry with my significant other he or she can forget about me being affectionate."

    Conditional Lover   or   Unconditional Lover

2. "We sometimes have to accept our significant others for who they are and not always attempt to change them."

    Conditional Lover   or   Unconditional Lover

3. "Having standards is okay, but we must also remember that no one is perfect. Too much emphasis is placed on physical attributes, status and other things that have nothing to do with real love."

    Conditional Lover   or   Unconditional Lover

4. "I can't be with someone who does not represent me well. Hard work is respectable, but status is more important."

    Conditional Lover   or   Unconditional Lover

5. "I have been hurt before and now I have a list of conditions a person must meet before I let my guard down. I am afraid of getting hurt so my future mate will have to work hard to win me over."

Conditional Lover   or   Unconditional Lover

6. "Often we fail to realize that relationships should be built on love and respect, not perfectionist tendencies. It does not make sense to withdraw or limit love because you are not happy."

Conditional Lover   or   Unconditional Lover

7. "If we loved each other like God loves us. We would strive to love others despite their shortcomings."

Conditional Lover   or   Unconditional Lover

8. "I give the most when I am happy. If I am upset I do not give as easily. My spouse knows that I only give plentifully when I am happy."

Conditional Lover   or   Unconditional Lover

9. "I love to influence others not to control them."

Conditional Lover   or   Unconditional Lover

10. "Loving without limits leads to trouble. People love best when they feel like they have something to lose."

Conditional Lover   or   Unconditional Lover

-----------------------Unconditional Love-----------------------

ANSWERS:

1.) Conditional Lover
2.) Unconditional Lover
3.) Unconditional Lover
4.) Conditional Lover
5.) Conditional Lover
6.) Unconditional Lover
7.) Unconditional Lover
8.) Conditional Lover
9.) Unconditional Lover
10.) Conditional Lover

How do love styles develop?

The way in which we give and receive love can be best understood by exploring the three most influential factors that affect our beliefs and actions about receiving and giving love: family teachings or observations, previous relationship experiences and societal perceptions.

Family Teachings or Observations

If you desire to learn how an individual's love style developed, simply inquire about his or her childhood experiences. We are all by-products of our total life experiences, including childhood experiences. Too often, children are taught directly or indirectly that love must be reciprocal. As a result they struggle to love themselves and others when they do not feel loved.

Our first exposure to interpersonal relationships comes from family interactions. Through direct involvement or observation we learn certain skills and habits, including how to receive and give love. Regardless of the method, we initially develop love styles from our family members. Most individuals would like to think they love the way they do based on personal experiences alone, but this is not true. We have all been impacted by family experiences in some form or fashion.

Children who grew up in households where love was expressed freely and without hesitation are likely to become adults who express love freely and without hesitation. The process of learning how to give and receive love is strongly influenced by the adults in a child's life. For example, if a child witnessed his or her parent express love when he or she was pleased or happy, the child may have learned that love is shared only under pleasant conditions or circumstances. On the other hand, if a child witnessed his or her parent express love when he or she was dissatisfied or unhappy, the child may have learned that love is shared regardless of conditions or circumstances.

If an individual was abused, observed abuse, received inadequate love or was deprived of love during their childhood, it is highly likely that he or she will be emotionally guarded as an adult. Some clients I have worked with, who have experienced abuse in their childhood, have expressed difficulty with receiving and giving love unconditionally. Others developed poor boundaries and expressed that they often gave too much of themselves to compensate for the love they did not receive in their childhood. For many, childhood experiences have taught them that one must guard their heart to prevent suffering or love freely to experience the benefits of loving unconditionally.

Different love styles can potentially cause conflict in relationships because individuals from different backgrounds frequently experience and express love differently. Discussions about childhood upbringing can provide vital information about the development of an individual's love style. The behaviors and customs that individuals present in adulthood were shaped over a period of time. Understanding their foundation is vital to having a clear picture of how they give and receive love.

Different love styles can potentially cause conflict in relationships because individuals from different backgrounds frequently experience and express love differently.

Examples:

Jimmy: "My childhood was okay. My parents' relationship was good and bad. When they were happy with each other the house was filled with love. However, when they were unhappy or angry with each other the house was filled with tension. If my mother was upset with my father she made him sleep on the couch and talked harsh to him; if my father was upset with my mother he was mean toward her and attempted to limit her independence. I assumed they placed these conditions on each other in an attempt to control behavior. From my childhood experience, I learned to give love during positive situations and limit love during negative or tense situations. In my current marriage, I often find myself expressing love when I am in a good mood or happy. I never assumed that my childhood experience had such as an effect on how I give and receive love. I guess I learned to love based on conditions."

Conditional Lover or Unconditional Lover

Michele: "My parents had disagreements like any other couple. My father was not happy with my mother's frequent shopping sprees. They fought and argued frequently, but their love for each other did not alter. My father told me that he learned early in life that people cannot be controlled. He was upset with my mother and wanted her to stop shopping, but did not outwardly express his frustration or limit his love. Instead he set down with my mother, reviewed bank statements with her and expressed how he felt. He helped her understand that her spending habits were negatively affecting their ability to plan for the future. My mother told me that it was difficult to stop spending money freely, but she worked hard because my father did not try to control her. She appreciated that he was patient with her and did not place conditions on her. From my childhood experience, I learned that it is best to try to influence others' behavior. Love has nothing to do with controlling others."

Conditional Lover or Unconditional Lover

Previous Relationship Experiences

Childhood experience may strongly influence one's love style, but does not solely determine it. Through relationships with others as adults the love style we developed in childhood can be sustained or altered. Positive and healthy past relationships contribute to an individual's willingness to express love unconditionally and without fear. However, negative and unhealthy past relationship can contribute to an individual's unwillingness to express love unconditionally.

Past failed relationships may have long-term negative effects on individuals if they lack healthy coping skills. A damaged heart and loss of trust is difficult to repair. Some individuals learn and grow in a

-----------------------Unconditional Love-----------------------

positive manner from failed relationships; while others become victims who allow pain and suffering to destroy their desire to give and receive unconditional love. Seeking to understand an individual's previous relationship experiences can offer useful information in regards to understanding his or her love style.

Examples:

June: "I was married for ten years and gave my all to my husband. I do not know why my husband left. Some people can't appreciate anything or anyone. I am not giving my all again. Whoever I date in the future will have to work really hard to earn my love. My previous pain reminds me of the importance of shielding my heart from others. My friends tell me that I will never find true love by doing so, but I do not care." Conditional Lover or Unconditional Lover

Sam: "My relationship with my ex-wife did not work, but I enjoyed our time together. Over the course of our five year marriage we learned that we were different. Her values were different than mind and we argued too much. We loved each other, but could not make it work. I gave what I thought was my all, but apparently it was not enough to save my marriage. It hurt me really bad to see my marriage end, but I am not afraid to love again. I forgave my wife for everything she did to me and prayed that she would forgive me for the things I did to her." Conditional or Unconditional Lover

Societal Perceptions

Societal perceptions regarding how women and men should love also contribute to the development of love styles. Women are perceived to be sensitive individuals who are expected to sacrifice their happiness to please others. In contrast, men are perceived to be sensitively challenged individuals who are expected to put their needs before others. Throughout history both women and men have accepted these perceptions as fact. It is unfortunate that such perceptions penetrate to the core of our society. Childrearing and adult relationships are influenced by these societal views. Given the differences in perceptions, one would assume that in comparison to men, women are more likely to embrace unconditional love as their love style. Over the course of my career as a therapist I have witnessed thousands of women do whatever they can to give and receive love; even put others' needs before their own. In fact, eighty-five percent of the couples' therapy sessions I have conducted were initiated by women. I make this distinction not to say that women cannot be conditional lovers, but to point out that women are more likely to embrace characteristics of an unconditional lover. Under-standing your love style also requires an understanding of societal perceptions. Furthermore, if you desire to learn more about your significant others' love style, explore his or her ideas about how women and men love and compare them to societal perceptions.

Now that you have a bettering understanding of different love styles and how they develop, do you feel good about your love style? You cannot change your childhood experiences, past relationships or societal perceptions, but you can change your love style. If you are a conditional lover and would like to transform into an unconditional lover, there are two key strategies to follow:

1.) Establish a relationship with God

    a.   God will bless you with knowledge and wisdom that will enhance your understanding of the true meaning of unconditional love; He gave his only begotten son so that you can have a second chance at life and love. Redemption was granted not by your doing, but by the compassion and grace of God. Study the *Word* and learn to do what God has already done for you.

2.) Treat others as you would like to be treated – The Golden Rule

    a.   If you desire to be loved unconditionally, learn what it takes to love others unconditionally and strive to treat others the way you expect to be treated. You may struggle to relate to others at times, but put yourself in their shoes and respond to them in the same manner you would want or expect them to respond to you.

Lack of understanding about different love styles can lead to a life full of unproductive relationships and unhappiness. You need to be aware of your love style and be willing to modify it if you desire to have a relationship filled with unconditional love. Combining your new knowledge with strategies you will learn in the following chapters will guide the course of your relationships for years to come. In the second section of this book, I present R.E.A.L. strategies that you should master in order to be successful at giving and receiving unconditional love in your relationship.

"Love is a gift from God, but you determine your style"

What's your love style?
Who or what influenced your love style?
Do feel you can or need to change your style of love?
Why or Why not?

_____
_____
_____
_____
_____
_____
_____
_____
_____
_____
_____
_____
_____
_____
_____
_____
_____
_____
_____
_____
_____
_____

----------------------Unconditional Love----------------------

PART TWO

HOW TO GIVE AND RECEIVE UNCONDITIONAL LOVE

4

The R.E.A.L. Concept

In previous chapters I defined love, unconditional love and discussed their functions. I also defined love styles and how they develop. This chapter provides you with a concept that will empower you to apply the knowledge you have acquired about unconditional love. Proper knowledge about love is paramount to having healthy relationships. However, possessing knowledge is not beneficial unless it can be applied in your relationship. To assist you with this undertaking, I developed the R.E.A.L. concept and have found it to be instrumental in helping individuals give and receive unconditional love.

The R.E.A.L. Concept

Each relationship is distinct and has its own unique challenges. The R.E.A.L. concept can be used as a tool to help you understand what unconditional love is and how to develop it in your relationship. The R.E.A.L. Concept is articulated as:

R – *Realistic* approach
E – Rational **E***xpectations*
A – Positive *Attitude*
L – *Love* unconditionally

The "R"

The R encourages you to approach situations in a *Realistic* manner. It is important to express an awareness of things as they really are but use sound judgment and demonstrate empathy. Also seek to understand the source of problems before you attempt to address or solve them.

The "E"

The E encourages you to exercise sound reasoning in order to develop rational *Expectations* or beliefs. The expectations you have of yourself, others and life in general often reflect how you live your life. Eliminate irrational expectations and replace them with rational ones.

The "A"

The A encourages you to maintain a positive *Attitude* of yourself and others. Do not let your attitude or feelings prevent you from being happy or progressing in life. Negativity begets negativity. Change starts with you.

The "L"

The L encourages you to develop unconditional *Love* for yourself and others. Establish a deep, tender, indefinable feeling of affection and attentiveness toward yourself and others that is not determined or influenced by someone or something.

This concept provides a road map for giving and receiving unconditional love in your relationship. There can't be unconditional love in any relationship without the development and application of appropriate and healthy interpersonal skills. The R.E.A.L. approach is the best method of giving and receiving unconditional love. It encourages women and men to interact with each other in a respectful, empathic, nonjudgmental and positive manner.

The concept can be essential to saving and restoring troubled relationships, but successful application of the concept requires individuals to be intellectually and emotionally balanced. In order to approach situations realistically and develop rational expectations, you must be capable of thinking clearly and objectively. Additionally, to maintain a positive attitude and develop unconditional love, you must be capable of feeling wholeheartedly and subjectively. Giving and receiving unconditional love is possible if you use the R.E.A.L. concept, but be aware of self-preserving personality traits that can prevent and limit you from using the concept successfully in your relationship.

SELF-PRESERVING PERSONALITY TRAITS

At points in our lives we rely on certain personality traits more than others and learn to use traits that are common to us or appear to reap the greatest benefit for us. I have observed that both women and men are primarily driven by one or two distinctive, but domineering self-preserving personality traits: "The Emotional Me Trait" or "The Intellectual Me Trait".

The Emotional Me Trait

The "Emotional Me Trait" is an expressive trait that enables individuals to communicate how they feel. The trait receives fuel from the heart and is mainly operated by feelings. Individuals, who utilize this trait frequently, often believe that feelings are as equally important or more important than facts. Subjectivity or emotionality play a vital role in how they make decisions and experience life. Expressing sensitive and nurturing emotions and giving of self freely is valued, encouraged and praised. However, individuals who are dominated by this personality trait have difficulty understanding and connecting reason and emotion. Their emotions either block or limit

-----------------------Unconditional Love-----------------------

49

their ability to view or comprehend things rationally. They speak and behave based on how they feel. Their intellectual capacity is not necessarily inadequate, but is dominated by emotions. They will endure prolonged suffering to preserve their "Emotional Me Trait".

The "Emotional Me Trait" has created emotional distress and confusion for many women and men. I have personally witnessed individuals engage in demoralizing and self-inhibiting behavior in an attempt to preserve their "Emotional Me Trait". For example; remaining in emotionally and/or physically abusive relationships because they would "feel" bad if they walked away; and refusing to seek help because they "feel" they can resolve their own problem or would "feel" bad if someone knew their relationship was troubled. This profound desire to preserve and nurture the "Emotional Me Trait" has proven to be detrimental to women's and men's emotional and physical health.

Women and men have a deep need to be loved, especially unconditionally and will often accept and tolerate "nonsense" in a relationship as long as they "feel" loved. The "Emotional Me Trait" occasionally prevents women and men from approaching situations in a *Realistic* manner and developing rational *Expectations*. This in turn contributes to their inability to apply the R.E.A.L. concept successfully in their relationship.

The Intellectual Me Trait

The "Intellectual Me Trait" is a thought provoking trait that enables individuals to communicate what they think. The trait receives fuel from the psyche and is mainly operated by intellect. Individuals, who utilize this trait frequently, often believe that facts are as equally important or more important than emotions. Objectivity or impartiality play a vital role in how they make decisions and experience life. Expression of sensitive and nurturing emotions and giving freely of self is calculated and executed with apprehension and foresight. Individuals who are dominated by this personality trait have difficulty understanding and connecting emotion and reason. Their intellect either blocks or limits their ability to view or comprehend things emotionally. They speak and behave based on how they think. Their emotional capacity is not necessarily inadequate, but is dominated by intellect.

The "Intellectual Me Trait" enables individuals to guard their hearts from emotional pain. However, it also contributes to the emotional distance that usually manifest in their relationships. I have personally witnessed individuals engage in inappropriate verbal confrontations in an attempt to preserve their "Intellectual Me Trait". They rely heavily on their intellect to cope with and understand life challenges. If they are forced to deal with emotions, they are likely to become frustrated when their intellect fails them. Individuals who rationalize everything typically have difficulty feeling wholeheartedly and subjectively, thus causing others to categorize them as negative individuals who do not love unconditionally.

The "Intellectual Me Trait" can prevent women and men from maintaining a positive *Attitude* and developing unconditional *Love* if they fail to understand or comprehend something intellectually. This in turn contributes to their inability to apply the R.E.A.L. concept successfully in their relationship.

To bond with and express unconditional love for your significant other, it is necessary that you understand *love styles* highlighted in chapter three and *self-preserving personality traits* highlighted above. In doing so, you can gain insight that will help you cope with differences between you and your partner more effectively. As mentioned in chapter three, love styles are developed based on family teachings or observations, previous relationship experiences and societal views. The same factors also influence the development of self-preserving personality traits as well. Similar to your love style, your self-preserving personality trait strongly influences how you express love.

During my investigation of how to help women and men give and receive unconditional love, I discovered that love styles and self-preserving personality traits definitely affect how individuals give and receive unconditional love. I also discovered that there are two categories of conditional lovers and two categories of unconditional lovers. Let's look at each category.

Intellectual Conditional Lover (ICL)
Versus
Emotional Conditional Lover (ECL)

Intellectual Conditional Lover (ICL)

You give and receive love based on intellectual aptitude. You need to be stimulated intellectually or you lose interest. Intelligence is very appealing and attractive to you. You will give love if your significant other meets your intellectual need. However, if your significant other is not capable of intellectualizing like yourself, you withdraw or limit your love to protect your heart.

Emotional Conditional Lover (ECL)

You give and receive love based on emotional aptitude. You need to be stimulated emotionally or you lose interest. You will share your emotions freely as long as you are receiving what you put out. However, if your significant other is incapable of meeting your emotional needs, you withdraw or limit your love to protect your heart.

Intellectual Unconditional Lover (IUCL)
Versus
Emotional Unconditional Lover (EUCL)

Intellectual Unconditional Lover (IUCL)

You give and receive love based on intellectual aptitude, but do not withdraw or limit your love if your significant other is not capable of doing the same. You search for commonalities and learn to appreciate your significant other for who he or she is. You strive to enhance your significant other's intellectual capacity, but do not force him or her to view the world through your intellectual lens.

------------------------The R.E.A.L. Concept------------------------

Emotional Unconditional Lover (EUCL)

You give and receive love based on emotional aptitude, but do not withdraw or limit your love if your significant other is not capable of doing the same. You explore options to help him or her comprehend the importance of good emotional health. You understand that emotions are expressed in a variety of ways and strive to expand your understanding of your significant other's emotional "intelligence" while nurturing your emotional needs.

If you and your significant other are experiencing ongoing conflict over what appears to be trivial and solvable issues, it may be that you do not understand each other's dominate self-preserving personality trait or love style. Comprehension of the self-preserving traits outlined in this chapter along with love styles can help you better understand how you and your significant other express love and cope with adversity differently in your relationship. Depending on what is happening in your relationship and your comfort level, you might rely heavily on one trait. However, to successfully apply the concept in your relationship you must learn to balance both traits. God created humans, both women and men, with the ability to "feel" and "think" because He understood the importance of balance. As the saying goes, too much of anything is not healthy. There is a time to think, a time to feel and a time to do both.

Allowing one of the two self-preserving personality traits to dominate you is not beneficial for you or your significant other. If your dominant trait is different than your significant other, make time to learn about his or her trait and practice incorporating it into your relationship. Don't ignore, minimize or attempt to change it. Learning to balance expression of self-preserving personality traits is a critical skill that will enable you to succeed with accomplishing most tasks including implementation of this empowering concept in your relationship. In the remaining chapters, you will learn how to balance your self-preserving personality traits and apply the R.E.A.L. Concept to develop and sustain the unconditional love you desire.

-----------------------Unconditional Love-----------------------

"Concepts have little significance unless they are applied effectively"

What challenges do you feel or think you will encounter as you attempt to implement the R.E.A.L Concept in your relationship? What can you do to apply the concept effectively in your relationship?

What is your Self-Preserving Personality Trait (SPPT)? What is your significant other's SPPT?

_____

_____

_____

_____

_____

_____

_____

_____

_____

_____

_____

_____

_____

_____

5

Strategy #1:

Be Realistic

Relationships are 1% Love and 99% Work

Most people enter into relationships with the intent of living happily ever after, but do not realize or want to accept the fact that relationships are 1% love and 99% work. You are probably saying that no relationship can last forever if love plays such a small role. I previously thought the same, but have learned different. If love alone was enough to maintain relationships the current divorce rate would not be at 50% and climbing. Relationships do not endure because of love, but because of the work that is invested to nurture love. The ability to give and receive unconditional love requires you to take action. If you learn nothing else about relationships, remember that they are 1% Love and 99% Work.

Relationships are 1% Love

The exhilarating feeling of being in love typically lasts eighteen months to two years, a time period in which most relationship experts refer to as the "honeymoon stage". During this timeframe individuals go out of their way to please each other. Apologizing for

------------------------Unconditional Love------------------------

mistakes is common just as gifts and surprises for birthdays and anniversaries come without reminders or requests. "I Love You" is repeated numerous times throughout the day and even in the presence of others. Physical and emotional affection is abundant. Sexual encounters are spontaneous, exciting and viewed as being mind blowing because the heart is well positioned.

Thoughts of being with the other person run rampantly through individuals' minds daily. "I am so in love with you" is said with enthusiasm. No wrongs are worth arguing over during this time period. Difficult to cope with qualities such as stubbornness and inflexibility are minimized or are addressed in a positive and patient manner. Personality and value differences are viewed as strengths instead of obstacles. Individuals often state, "Where I am weak, you are strong. This is why our relationship is so wonderful". Loving each other unconditionally seems effortless and individuals question why they waited so long to feel so good.

The couple is soaring off of love and does not want to do anything to ruin their high. Love rules the relationship and feelings of inseparability are enough to persuade both individuals to support each other through the good and bad. Does any of this sound familiar? Everything that happens during this period strongly contributes to the 1% of love that exists in most relationships.

The exhilarating feeling of being in Love typically lasts eighteen months to two years.

Relationships are 99% Work

Love without work does not last. After the exhilarating feeling of being in love weakens, reality sets in and the dynamics of being in a committed relationship, to include; building and maintaining a life together, adjusting to career shifts, parental responsibilities, occasional in-law dilemmas and life stressors in general begin to take a toll on the relationship. Now individuals attempt to balance personal needs with their mates' needs, but find it difficult to do so at times. The hustle and bustle that comes with trying to secure and maintain the American dream and keeping a spouse, two kids and a dog happy, leaves little time to express physical, sexual and emotional affection. Sexual encounters are scheduled, not as exciting and viewed as being part of marital obligation. Complacency sets in and "I Love You is *replaced* with "You know I love you, I should not have to say it all the time".

Difficult to cope with qualities such as stubbornness and inflexibility are seen as such and are typically addressed in a negative or belittling manner. Personality and value differences are viewed as obstacles instead of strengths. Individuals often state, "We are so different and this is why we have so many problems in our relationship". Striving to love each other unconditionally is exhausting and leads some to question why they rushed to get involved in a relationship. Depending on the intensity and number of stressors in the relationship, one or both individuals might say, "I love you, but I am not in love with you anymore".

Love is still present, but is slowly fading. Thoughts of the relationship potentially ending influence both individuals to do what is best for self. Both individuals realize that work is needed if the relationship is to survive. Does this sound familiar? Everything that happens during this period accounts for the 99% of work that is required to maintain most relationships.

Love without work does not last

Now that I have explained my theory, let's test your knowledge about relationships. Answer the true and false questions below.

1) Good intentions with poor communication can sustain relationships. True or False

2) If love is present in the relationship, work is not needed. True or False

3) Love only fades when serious problems are present in relationships. True or False

-----------------------Unconditional Love-----------------------

59

4) People maintain happy relationships by working to satisfy each other. True or False

5) Any relationship worth having is worth working for. True or False

Continue reading for the answers.

Why is it important to comprehend the 1% Love - 99% Work Relationship Theory?

It is important for individuals to be aware of what typically happens in relationships from beginning to end. Bad relationships usually do not occur overnight. Generally speaking, a large percent of relationships fail due to a lack of work, not love. Love is definitely needed in any relationship that will endure for any period of time; however, love is simply an emotion that has no meaning unless something is done to sustain it. My 1% Love and 99% Work Relationship Theory was derived from sessions with married couples. In session after session I would hear women and men say that marriage requires a great deal of work; even happy marriages. To better understand the reason why so many couples felt this way, I began to track and document their responses. The results revealed the following:

1) Women and men view marriage and committed relationships as social institutions that require individuals to cooperate or comply with certain rules or expectations. Each individual enters the institution/relationship with preset core values or standards that define appropriate and inappropriate behavior. Value differences are either unrecognized or ignored in the beginning of most relationships because individuals believe that value differences should not be problematic for individuals who are deeply in love. Well these differences can be problematic. Why?

--------------------------Be Realistic--------------------------

60

2) Unfortunately, a large percent of individuals who get married or enter into relationships do not share similar *core values* or *are not willing to work to establish them*. Values are traits that are considered worthwhile and represent an individual's highest priorities and deeply held driving forces. Value differences in relationships mean that additional work is necessary to coexist in harmony.

Do you have friends or family members who are experiencing difficulty in their relationships because of value differences?

Establishing and maintaining relationships is fundamental to human existence. Relationships enable individuals to bond with others and fulfill their need for intimacy. The need to grow and connect with another person is the primary reason that we seek to develop relationships. Unfortunately, we enter relationships with individuals only to find out later that their core values are completely different than ours. How and why does this happen? It is usually due to physical proximity, similarities and physical attractiveness. Let's review all three.

Physical proximity is important because as humans we have a tendency to bond with individuals who are physically close to us. Familiarity and opportunity are underlying motives for establishing relationships based on physical proximity. The more you are around a person the more the person is likely to "grow" on you. Frequent contacts can enhance positive feeling toward another individual.

Next, similarities are also influential in determining whether one will enter into a relationship. You bond with individuals that appear to share similar goals, entertainment and social preferences, and beliefs as yourself. Similarity helps individuals feel comfortable and reduces distress and tension. For example, individuals typically report the following: "We like to do the same things. We go out to eat, socialize with friends, dance, travel, etc." However, when asked about similarities in regards to communicating, respect and trust, individuals usually express significant differences.

Lastly, physical attraction is the third reason someone decides to enter into a relationship. Individuals are initially attracted to others based on their physical appearance. This is very prevalent in our society because physical attractiveness is rewarded. Individuals who are very attractive are usually popular and receive more attention than less attractive people.

While all three reasons factor significantly in the decision to enter a relationship, I believe that a relationship will be troubled if core values are not similar. When getting to know an individual, physical attraction and proximity sets the stage. Physical attraction initially influences your desire to approach another person and physical proximity gives you an opportunity to meet and interact with him or her. If you discover that the other person has similar interests, you are encouraged to pursue the relationship. Similarities set the stage for intimate relationships to develop. Individuals, who appear to share similar interests and beliefs, are more likely to enter into an intimate relationship. However, dissimilarity in core values will cause conflict. I have provided counseling to hundreds of couples who were troubled because they did not share similar core values about communication, money management, expression of emotions and other issues that affect the quality of relationships. Interpersonal similarities are needed to develop a relationship, but similar core values are needed to sustain it.

Many individuals marry or enter relationships because of physical attraction and superficial similarities, but give little thought to the importance of sharing similar core values. In my opinion, the ability to give and receive unconditional love is easier for individuals who share similar core values or are willing to develop them. If physical attraction and superficial similarities was enough, individuals would have long and prosperous relationships and the institute of marriage would not be in jeopardy. However, this is not the case. The institute of marriage is steadily eroding because physical appearance and superficial similarities are being used as foundational cornerstones. Before you decide to enter a relationship or get married be aware that every person has values that influence his or her behavior. Make sure that your core values are compatible with theirs or be willing to work to develop them. No other social institution is affected by the lack of similarities in core values like the institute of marriage. The best marriages have two individuals who are dedicated to working and developing similar core values.

Many individuals marry or enter relationships because of physical attraction and superficial similarities, but give little thought to the importance of sharing similar core values.

The Institution of Marriage

Marriage is a beautiful union and can bring a wealth of joy if the "right" kind of work is conducted to sustain it. In the past two years, I have attended four weddings and experienced mixed feelings each time I heard the minister facilitate the exchange of vows. One side of me was filled with gladness and optimism while the other side was filled with sadness and pessimism. On one occasion I questioned whether both individuals truly understood the seriousness of what they had just agreed to. The exchange occurred as follows:

Minster - Do you John Williams take Susan Johnson to be your wife – to live together after God's ordinance – in the holy estate of matrimony? Will you love her, comfort her, honor and keep her, in sickness and in health, for richer, for poorer, for better, for worse, in sadness and in joy, to cherish and continually bestow upon her your heart's deepest devotion, forsaking all others, keep yourself only unto her as long as you both shall live?

John Williams-I will.

Minster- Do you Susan Johnson take John Williams to be your husband – to live together after God's ordinance – in the holy estate of matrimony? Will you love him, comfort him, honor and keep him, in sickness and in health, for richer, for poorer, for better, for worse, in sadness and in joy, to cherish and continually bestow upon him your heart's deepest devotion, forsaking all others, keep yourself only unto him as long as you both shall live?

-----------------------Unconditional Love-----------------------

63

Susan Johnson-I will.

After hearing the vows, my joyful and optimistic side was convinced that love and good intention would help the couple remain committed to their vows. On the other hand, my worried and pessimistic side was convinced that love alone will not help the couple remain committed to their vows. As I explored my ambivalence, I realized that I felt pessimism because I had conversed and interacted with hundreds of individuals who had repeated the same vows only to walk away from the marriages when things were not going well.

In my experience as a therapist, I have found that individuals find it easy to love and honor their spouse when they are healthy, financially stable, and joyful. However, I have found that the same individuals restrict or limit their love and dishonor their spouse when they are sick, financially or emotionally unstable or experience periods of sadness. For this reason I do not think that love alone is enough to help individuals remain committed to their vows. When things get rough, as they will, love and a working attitude must be present to sustain the relationship.

Marriage vows were written with a function component that addresses the good and bad in relationships. I believe they were written as they are to remind individuals that relationships require work. It is frequently said that individuals work for what they want. Unfortunately, this exemplary work ethic appears to apply to every aspect of life except in intimate personal relationships. It saddens me to see how easily individuals move from relationship to relationship when they are unhappy. Marriages, like other social institutions, grow and prosper when individual team players are committed to investing quality time and energy into preserving it.

The military has endured much turmoil for several decades but has had much success in motivating individuals to remain committed to the institution. How? As individuals enter the military they are required to take an oath. The oath, like a marriage vow, is a commitment to the institution and reads as follows:

--------------------------------Be Realistic--------------------------

64

I, _____, do solemnly swear (or affirm) that I will support and defend the Constitution of the United States against all enemies, foreign and domestic; that I will bear true faith and allegiance to the same; that I take this obligation freely, without any mental reservation or purpose of evasion; and that I will well and faithfully discharge the duties of the office on which I am about to enter. So help me God.

While many claim to understand the meaning of their marriage vows, very few are capable of upholding them during difficult times. Similar to the military oath, marriage vows provide the framework for expected and desired behavior of members in the institution. In order to preserve the institution, unity and harmony must be present. What does this mean and how can it be accomplished?

During rough times in their relationships, individuals frequently engage in behavior that will potentially advance their personal interests, thus causing disharmony in the institution. This self-preserving behavior is a natural response to disorderliness, but often places personal interests above what is important to preserving the institution. Selfish and self-centered behavior is the primary reason for the failure of most marriages and relationships. So in order to preserve the institution, behavior must be consistent and have shared significance to each member in the institution. This is referred to as "harmonizing" and can be accomplished by establishing core values.

Military leaders realized that the oath alone, like marriage vows is too difficult to uphold during difficult times, so core values were designed to guide the behavior of all members in the institution. Core values inspire each member to do his or her best to preserve the institution and remind individuals of their commitment when faced with adversity. Core values are constant when everything is wavering and changing. As a member of the United States Air Force for nearly a decade, I can attest that I learned to appreciate the importance of core values such as: Integrity First, Service before Self and Excellence in All We Do. I believe that you can apply these core values in your marriage or relationship and experience the uniformity and connectivity that the military has sustained and enjoyed for decades. Let's explore this further.

Integrity First – means to act in a righteous manner even when no one is looking. A person of integrity is honest, courageous, responsible, open, humble, accountable and respectful of self.

- Honest - your word is your bond. Lying is not an option.
- Courageous - you do what is right even if the cost is high.
- Responsible – accept your duties and perform them responsibly
- Open – you seek feedback to ensure you are performing your duties satisfactorily
- Humble – you embrace your duties with humility and strive to do your best
- Accountable – you accept responsibility for your actions and do not take credit for others
- Self-respect – behave in a manner that will not harm the reputation of self

What does Integrity First mean to you? Do you display it in your marriage or relationship? Why or Why not?

_____
_____
_____
_____
_____
_____
_____
_____
_____
_____
_____
_____
_____

--------------------------Be Realistic--------------------------

Here's what it means to me:

A person of integrity will uphold their marriage vows, walk away from an adulterous sexual advances or opportunities, accept his or her duties as a husband or wife, solicit feedback from their spouse or others in order to perform his or her duties satisfactorily, remain humble, accept responsibility for his or her actions and respect self at all times.

An individual of integrity is honest, courageous, responsible, open, humble, accountable and respectful of self.

Service before Self – means that one is willing to put his or her personal goals or desires on hold or adapt goals that will satisfy self-interests and advance the goals of the institution.

- Selflessness – you do what is best for the betterment of the institution, not just self
- Flexible – you learn to incorporate personal goals into selfless goals that strengthen the institution, not weaken it
- Discipline and Controlled – you do not indulge in self-pity, anger, discouragement, frustration or defeatism. You lead with an optimistic attitude and mindset.

What does Service before Self mean to you? Do you display it in your marriage or relationship? Why or Why not?

_____
_____
_____
_____
_____
_____
_____
_____

----------------------------Be Realistic----------------------------

Here's what it means to me:

A person who embraces service before self will not allow his or her pride or personal agenda prevent him or her from doing what is best for his or her marriage; will seek opportunities to strengthen his or her marriage by incorporating personal goals with marital goals; gives because it is the right thing to do, not because there is a return; and, accepts life challenges without feeling sorry for self, displaying anger, frustration, discouragement or defeatism. He or she embraces what it means to compromise, but also realizes that he or she will have to occasionally sacrifice to preserve the institution.

An individual who embraces service before self is willing to put his or her personal goals or desires on hold or adapt goals that satisfy self-interests and advance the marriage.

Excellence in All We Do – means to develop or maintain a passion for continuous growth and improvement that will drive the institution into a long-term, upward spiral of achievement and performance.

- Personal excellence – you engage in activities that will enhance your spiritual, physical and mental capabilities
- Mutual respect – you treat others with respect regardless of their attributes

What does Excellence in all We Do mean to you? Do you display it in your marriage or relationship? Why or Why not?

_____
_____
_____
_____
_____
_____
_____

--------------------------Be Realistic--------------------------

70

Here's what it means to me:

A person who embraces excellence in all we do constantly looks for opportunities to improve his or her marriage and self; believes that complacency and mediocrity is unacceptable; welcomes challenges and problems as opportunities to excel; and understands that each person is unique and can contribute if guided correctly.

An individual who embraces Excellence in All We Do develops or maintains a passion for continuous growth and improvement that will drive the marriage into a long-term, upward spiral of achievement and performance.

On the day that you recite your marriage vows or commit to a serious relationship, you have a strong desire to do what is right and hope that your union will last forever. You feel that your struggles are a thing of the past and that love will propel your relationship to the next level. However, lack of compatible core values will destroy or create distress in your relationship. If you desire to give and receive unconditional love in your relationship, work to establish similar core values if they do not already exist.

Values form the foundation for everything that happens in your relationship. Whatever values you hold will inundate your relationship. You will experience continued hardship if your values differ significantly from your significant other. If you are generally happy with your relationship, you probably selected a spouse who shares core values that are congruent with your own. Conversely, if you're not happy in your relationship, watch for dissimilarity between what you value and what your spouse values. Be mindful that no two individuals are the same, there are no perfect matches and love, like anything else in life, is expressed differently and shifts based on circumstances. Be realistic and prepare to work in order to give and receive the unconditional love you desire in your relationship. Seek to understand the source of your relational conflict then use sound judgment and demonstrate empathy to address it. If you desire to give and receive unconditional love, you have to devote time and energy—***work at it!***

--------------------------Be Realistic--------------------------

72

"Living in reality is better than fantasy because it prepares you to respond in a realistic manner"

Do you have a clear understanding of love and how it works? Do you fantasize, but fail to see relationships for what they are? Do you believe that relationships require work? Why or Why not?

_____

----------------------Unconditional Love----------------------

6

Strategy #2:

Develop Rational Expectations

"Expectations Guide Behavior"

Developing rational expectations is the second strategy that will enable you to give and receive unconditional love in your relationship. What you expect from your relationship is typically what you give. The expectations you have of yourself and others often reflect how you behave in your relationship. Do you enter relationships hoping to receive unconditional love, but have no intention to truly give it? Do you want individuals to love you for who you are, but put on a façade because of personal shortcomings or flaws? Do you enter relationships thinking that love will conquer all? If you answered yes, you need to evaluate your expectations. Evaluating your expectations is critical to being able to give and receive unconditional love. Expectations are powerful and can predispose you to certain experiences. Irrational expectations often cause or contribute to inappropriate expression of emotions and behavior. While rational expectations often cause or contribute to appropriate expression of emotions and behavior. You should make every effort to learn the difference. Let's review.

Expect To Give

Give is an action verb which means to put into the possession of another for his or her use. For God so loved the world that He gave His only begotten Son, that whoever believes in Him should not perish, but have eternal life (John 3:16). Some people are takers and some are givers. What kind of person are you? Do you give with a cheerful heart or out of obligation or guilt? Individuals who give with a cheerful heart understand the value of giving and the meaning of "Reap What You Sow". If you give conditional love you will most likely receive conditional love. However, if you give unconditional love you will almost certainly receive unconditional love.

Individuals who give with a cheerful heart understand the value of giving and the meaning of "Reap What You Sow".

It is irrational to expect to receive unconditional if you are not willing to give it. If you are a Christian I hope that you strive to give unconditional love like God does. No relationship can survive if only one person is giving. We all have a desire to receive, but routinely place too much emphasis on receiving and fail to appreciate the power of giving. Giving empowers you. Do not focus on the return because you cannot control what it will be. Instead give unconditional love and pray that it influences others to do the same.

Expect To Accept Your Significant Other for Who They Are

Entering a relationship and expecting to change your significant other will cause more problems in your relationship than you can ever imagine. Understand that most people just want to be accepted for who they are. Attempts to change others frequently contribute to feelings of resentment and bitterness. Recognize that what you believe is right for someone does not matter unless they agree. This is important to understand because you must realize that change will not occur or last unless your significant other can identify with the requested change and personally embrace it. If individuals are persuaded to do things they do not have a desire to do, most likely they will grow resentful or bitter, especially if the outcome does not meet their expectations. I realize that it is difficult to accept individuals as they are, especially when flaws are visible and appear to be destructive or self-inhibiting. However, individuals are more open to change if they feel that they are accepted despite their shortcomings.

True acceptance means to acknowledge positive and negative traits. A quick way to distance yourself from your significant other is to embrace his or her strengths and complain about his or her weaknesses. Have you ever observed how quickly your mood shifts after someone tells you that you are not good at something or does not offer positive support? If you do not agree with or dislike something about your significant other, offer support and provide positive criticism. While no criticism is easy to accept, positive criticism at least focuses on building a person's spirit. Capitalize on their good qualities while addressing negative qualities. It is easier for others to respond to your desires or wishes when they are not placed in a defensive mode.

It is irrational to expect that you can change another person. Change is a personal phenomenon and occurs when individuals are ready to change. Learn to listen to your significant other, be patient and let him or her know that you believe in them. In your quest to give and receive unconditional love become skilled at accepting your significant other for who he or she is. God did not create perfect people; therefore you, like others have both good and bad qualities; its part of being imperfect human beings! Accept your significant other as is and witness the power of giving and receiving unconditional love.

Expect to have a Successful Relationship

Expect to succeed in your relationship and be prepared for adversity. Relationship distress can wear you down and cause you to feel helpless and hopeless. It seems like the more you try to be positive, things get worse and giving up is the rational thing to do. Frustration and disappointment occur in every relationship, but does not always indicate that the relationship is in serious trouble or must end. However, if you dwell on the negative aspects of your relationship it will likely lead to the development of a failure mentality. Your mind is powerful and it sets the stage for your performance. If you expect your relationship to fail, you interact with your significant other with uneasiness, low motivation and doubt. Such emotions hinder your ability to bond with your significant other and are highly associated with failed relationships. On the other hand, if you expect your relationship to succeed, you interact with your significant other with confidence, enthusiasm and certainty. These emotions are uplifting and are more often in successful relationships. Shifting your expectations from a failure mentality can lay the foundation for a promising relationship. Positive thoughts lead to positive behaviors, thus increasing the chances of success. Life offers no guarantees, but I can guarantee you that if you expect to fail, you probably will. If you fail, your relationship fails.

Believe that your relationship can be successful and do not dread adversity. Adversity builds resiliency, and resiliency is a precursor to success. Success can be defined either by the process or outcome. It is important to learn the difference. Sometimes you will go through things in your relationship in order to mature and grow. Although you do not desire to experience difficult times in your relationship, the experiences can be considered useful if you learn from them.

Adversity builds resiliency, and resiliency is a precursor to success.

It is irrational to expect that you can give and receive unconditional love in a relationship that you do not believe will succeed. You are capable of having a successful relationship if decide you want to make it work. Individuals who possess high levels of commitment and dedication often succeed in their endeavors. How committed and dedicated are you to making your relationship succeed? What obstacles are you willing to overcome to succeed in your relationship? Do not base the success of your relationship on where it is today. Look at what it took to get to this point. If you look close enough you might find that your relationship has lasted as long as it has because you wanted it to. As long as you have it in your heart to succeed, your relationship can withstand the test of time. Giving and receiving unconditional love will become second nature. However, if your relationship is in trouble, ask for help. "Ask and you shall receive, seek and you will find; knock and the door will be opened to you; for everyone who asks will receive, and anyone who seeks will find, and the door will be opened to those who knock" (Mathew 7:7-8). If you desire to succeed, turn to the One who can truly help you. Your desire to succeed in your relationship is achievable if you seek help!

Expect To Change

You cannot expect to give or receive unconditional love in your relationship unless you are willing to change. The change that I am speaking of does not mean that you must give up who you are. Change requires one to be flexible in his or her thinking and doing. Doing the same thing over and over and expecting a different outcome is irrational. If you are experiencing conflict in your relationship, develop a plan to conquer it. The problems you encounter in your relationship are partially your fault. It takes two to quarrel. Some of you walk around daily with a chip on your shoulder. You are mad at your significant other and treat him or her unkindly, but expect him or her to treat you with compassion. Does this make sense? Also, you expect your significant other to be sensitive to your needs and desires, but you fail to respond sensitively to theirs. This self-centeredness is the basis for conflict in most relationships. Search to find out what you can do differently or change about yourself to give and receive the unconditional love you desire.

Change requires one to be flexible in his or her thinking and doing. Doing the same thing over and over and expecting a different outcome is irrational.

It is irrational to expect that you can enter a relationship and remain the same. You cannot hold on to childhood teachings and previous relationship experiences, especially if they are not productive for you now. The combining of two lifestyles will bring forth change even if you do not want it. You cannot exist in a relationship and continue to think and act as if you are single. Changing yourself can prove to be beneficial to your well-being and your relationship.

Expect To Learn

Lack of knowledge destroys relationships. How do you expect to improve your relationship, if you lack knowledge? How often do you equip yourself with information that will help you solve or cope with hardships in your relationship? Your experience alone is not always the most effective way of learning. Vernon Law, a famous baseball player, once stated that, "Experience is a hard teacher because she gives the test first and the lesson afterwards." Instead of engaging in unhealthy relationships time after time and making the same mistakes, try equipping yourself with proper information before the test.

If you desire to give and receive unconditional love seek counseling and support if you are not successful. Develop a road map for enhancing your knowledge of yourself and your significant other. Learn to validate how your significant other feels, communicate effectively and resolve conflict appropriately. Trying to navigate through a relationship without proper directions or a map can lead to disaster. Matthew 15:14 says, "If the blind lead the blind, both shall fall in the ditch." How can you give and receive unconditional love when you do not know how? Empower yourself by acquiring knowledge and applying it. Lack of knowledge and irrational expectations are the root cause of most failed relationships.

It is irrational to expect that you can give and receive unconditional love in your relationship without equipping yourself with proper knowledge. You should consistently try to learn as much as you can about your significant other and healthy relationships. This means that you will utilize all available resources. Your willingness to grow and learn will ensure that your relationship will flourish and an abundance of unconditional love will follow.

Expect To Be Generous

Selfishness has no place in a relationship. Devotion to yourself will eventually cause you to be by yourself. Showing generosity to your significant other means that you are willing to share your heart and time. To share your heart requires you to express emotions. One of the biggest challenges for couples who have become complacent is their inability to share emotions. "You know how I feel- why do I have to tell you?" is commonly stated. This kind of thinking is counterproductive. Guarded or restricted emotional expression causes the most arguments in relationships. Emotional intimacy can only develop in a relationship when two hearts are joined. Sharing your heart requires you to express how you feel and not make assumptions. Emotions drive behavior so it is important to learn to understand and share your emotions in a positive manner. Lack of emotional capability not lack of intellectual capability causes conflict in relationships. Generosity reduces tension and can potentially influence your significant other to demonstrate the same behavior.

Devotion to yourself will eventually cause you to be by yourself!

Without a doubt no relationship can grow if individuals do not make time to talk and comfort each other. Telling your significant other that you love him or her is not enough. Most individuals believe what they see not what they hear. As the saying goes, "Action speaks louder than words". If you truly care about your partner you will make time to learn about and discuss his or her desires, challenges, joys and concerns. Individuals make time for people and things that are of value to them.

It is irrational to expect that you can give and receive unconditional love without being generous in your relationship. If you struggle to be generous toward your significant other, seek help. Giving of your heart and time is necessary to sustaining an emotionally healthy relationship. Never miss an opportunity to express what's in your heart. Furthermore, do not think that money can replace quality time in a relationship. You can replace money, but time is irreplaceable. If you find that generosity is not part of your relationship, then you should strive to develop it. Generosity can be taxing at times, but the reward is life changing.

Expect To Recognize and Praise Comprise and Sacrifice

Do you know the difference between compromise and sacrifice? Compromise requires you to meet your significant other in the middle. This approach is widely accepted and practiced in relationships because it positions each person to "win". Sacrifice requires you to give up something for the sole benefit of your significant other. This approach is not widely accepted or practiced because it positions one person to "win". Societal norms have contributed to the belief that women should be more willing to sacrifice than men. This unfortunate perception has caused tension in many relationships. We are no longer living in the 19th century. I would urge you to practice compromise and sacrifice if you desire to give and receive unconditional love.

At times in your relationship it will be most appropriate to compromise and at other times it will be most appropriate to sacrifice. If your significant other compromises or sacrifices, recognize and praise his or her effort. This is critical because recognition and praise contributes to gratifying feelings that lead to repeated behavior.

It is irrational to expect that you can give and receive unconditional love in your relationship if you are not willing to compromise and sacrifice. Giving of oneself and feeling good is not gender driven. Everyone desires to be recognized for his or her effort. Recognize that compromise and sacrifice is warranted in every relationship. Life events do not always transpire in perfect harmony. Therefore, you must be willing to compromise and sacrifice and honor your significant other for doing the same.

Expect To Be Vulnerable

Do you expect to be vulnerable in your relationship? This is a difficult question to answer because most people associate pain and heartache with being vulnerable and no one desires to be hurt. Many people view vulnerability as being defenseless. In general, vulnerability is perceived to be very negative. It leads to overwhelming feelings of fear in most people. For this reason, being vulnerable does not sound appealing because the risk is significant. However, you must realize that fear is a reality of life and must be conquered. "For God hath not given us the spirit of fear; but of power, and of love, and of a sound mind" (2 Timothy 1:7)". Relationships are risky, but you can have a satisfying experience if you plan accordingly and give unconditional love. People let their guards down and are more willing to face their fears when they feel comfortable. Loving your significant other unconditionally will enhance his or her confidence in the relationship. Only then being vulnerable will not seem so frightening.

It is irrational to expect that you can give and receive unconditional love in your relationship without being vulnerable. To truly experience unconditional love you must allow yourself to be vulnerable. Guarded hearts do not grow. In my opinion, allowing yourself to be vulnerable is a mark of true love. There is nothing wrong with being vulnerable-everyone hurts and is weak at some point in his or her life. Pretending to be strong all the time is not healthy and will eventually cause you more hardship in the long run. Learn to express the wide range of emotions God has given you.

"Your expectations set the stage for how you act in your relationship"

Why is important to develop rational expectations?
Can relationships survive if you and your significant other
have irrational expectations of each other?
Why or Why not?

_____
_____
_____
_____
_____
_____
_____
_____
_____
_____
_____
_____
_____
_____
_____
_____
_____
_____
_____

------------------------Unconditional Love------------------------

7

Strategy #3:

Maintain a Positive Attitude

"Remove Negativity from your Mind and Heart"

Maintaining a positive attitude is the third strategy to being able to give and receive unconditional love in your relationship. Your way of thinking affects every phase of your life, including your relationships. During my life, I have experienced many things and have been in and out of all kinds of relationships. Through those relationships, I have learned that there are two kinds of people: negative thinkers and positive thinkers. Positive thinkers often search for the good in their significant other and relationship. They are caring, confident, and respectful of others, as well as themselves. They have a strong desire to remove negativity from their mind, heart and relationship. Negative thinkers on the other hand, often search for the bad in their significant other and relationship. They are insensitive, unsure, and disrespectful. They seem to delight in drama and are unable to remove negativity from their mind, heart and relationship.

My life experiences have taught me that I cannot always control what happens to me, but I can control my attitude. It is easy to be negative when you are hurting, discouraged, and angry. Your inner critic makes it easy to criticize yourself, as well as others, especially when your desires or expectations are not met. It is only natural to want to attack those who hurt you, devalue you, belittle you, or contribute to your suffering. However, fighting fire with fire has never proven to be effective. Negativity begets to negativity.

Positive thinkers often search for the good in their significant other and relationship.

As human beings we are an adaptable species who have the capacity to physically or mentally will ourselves to cope with situations that create distress or conflict for us. When placed in situations that make us feel uncomfortable or threaten our psychological well-being, we search for ways to cope. If we are not capable of escaping distress by physical means, we attempt to change our attitudes. If inconsistencies exist among our attitudes and those of others, we experience conflict. In order to reduce this conflict we change our attitude to achieve a state of psychological balance. This explains the "negativity begets negativity" theory. Let me explain further.

If you are a positive person, but your significant other constantly presents a negative attitude day after day, you will eventually adopt the attitude of your significant other in order to reduce your emotional conflict. Extended and prolonged exposure to unpleasant stimuli causes individuals to adjust to their situation or environment in order to have psychological balance. It sounds irrational to think that someone will become negative to have peace, right? In an attempt to achieve and maintain a state of psychological balance, individuals will adopt the attitudes and behaviors of others. Given this, it important to watch the company you keep and monitor your attitude.

The attitude and behavior you exhibit daily will affect your relationships. Therefore, it is imperative that you remove negativity from your mind and heart. Look to explore and change negative attitudes and thoughts. What kind of thinker are you?

The key to giving and receiving unconditional love begins with your attitude. Dr. David Burns, MD proposed the theory of cognitive distortion. Cognitive distortions are inaccurate perceptions or thoughts that maintain negative thinking and emotions. Let's review some cognitive distortions that lead to negative attitudes. Among these distortions are:

Always/Never thinking

You think something that has happened will "always" reoccur, or you will "never" secure what you desire or want. For example, if your significant other fails to remember a special occasion, you might think "He or she always forgets about me and I never get what I want". This thought is negative and can cause you to hold a grudge and feel unappreciated.

It's Never My Fault/Blaming

You blame your significant other for hardships in your relationship and see yourself as a victim. You do not accept responsibility for your actions, emotions, or behavior because you feel that others caused them. For example, "I would have never hit you if you did not make me angry". "I withdraw my love because I have been hurt before so it is not my fault that you do not feel loved. I do the best I can"

Blame thinking prevents you from giving and receiving unconditional love because you blame others for your actions and emotions. "I can't love you the way I want to because my parents never showed me how to love." This kind of thinking restricts you from exercising your personal sense of power. Taking responsibility for your behavior empowers you to change it.

Mental Filter

You select a single negative experience and dwell on it exclusively until your view of reality is clouded. For example, your significant other purchases nice things for your birthday each year, but forgot one year. Instead of being happy and praising your spouse for all the times he or she remembered, you dwell on the one time he or she forgot, telling yourself that your significant other is insensitive. You have a tendency to filter out positive experiences.

Disqualifying the Positive

You dismiss positive experiences by insisting they do not count or matter. For example, your significant other does everything that he or she can possibly do to make you happy because they love you. But, because you do not feel lovable, you reject or minimize his or her efforts. This thinking allows you to maintain a negative belief that is contradicted by your everyday experiences.

Jumping to Conclusions

You randomly jump to a negative conclusion that is not justified by the facts of the situation. "Mind reading" and "Fortune Teller" are two examples of this kind of thinking.

- o Mind reading – you conclude that someone is reacting negatively to you, without checking the facts. "I know he or she does not like me. We have never talked and he or she does not speak to me."

- o Fortune Teller – you anticipate that things will turn out poorly and you are convinced that your prediction is an established fact. "Why should I try to date him or her? The relationship will not work anyway. It's a waste of my time."

Emotional Reasoning

You assume that your negative emotions automatically reflect the way things really are. "I feel it, therefore it must be true. I feel unlovable, therefore I must be unlovable." This kind of thinking restricts your ability to give and receive love because your feelings do not always reflect reality.

Labeling and Mislabeling

Instead of describing your mistake or inappropriate behavior, you attach a negative label to yourself. "I'm a bad spouse." When someone else's behavior rubs you the wrong way, you attach a negative label to him or her. "He or she's a bad person." Mislabeling is when you describe an event with language that is highly distorted and emotionally loaded. "I'm a failure" instead of "I made a mistake".

Personalization

You see yourself as the cause of some negative external event which, in fact, you were not primarily responsible for. This distortion is the primary cause of guilt feelings. For example, "It's my fault that my significant other committed adultery. I did whatever I could to please him or her; it's my fault that I did not do enough and he turned to someone else. I should have done more to prevent it from happening."

Are you guilty of using any of the cognitive distortions listed above? You are responsible for your attitude. Your view about giving and receiving unconditional love depends upon what you tell yourself, how you treat yourself, and how you understand your world.

It is important to pay attention to your attitude, especially negative attitudes that affect your relationships, work, and life in general. Recognizing and modifying negative attitudes early is the most effective way of reducing their impact. If you fail to address negative attitudes early, you begin to believe them, and inappropriate behavior will follow. While it is normal to protect yourself from being hurt, it is unhealthy to maintain negative attitudes. Unfortunately, most of you struggle to remove negative attitudes because they are deeply rooted in your belief systems. Sometimes you are unaware that you are being negative. For this reason, it is important to check your attitude before you respond to a situation or person.

By now you might be asking, "What does my attitude have to do with giving and receiving unconditional love?" I am glad you asked.

Negative attitudes can lead to distrust and apathy. Distrusting others often makes you feel like you cannot give love, which can lead to emotional and physical isolation. Apathy can cause you to have little compassion for yourself or others, which can also lead to emotional and physical isolation. You might find yourself questioning others' intentions and behavior without valid justification. You might unconsciously distance yourself emotionally and overreact to small challenges. You might enter into a relationship or engage in sex, but detach emotionally to prevent yourself from being hurt. You might stay in a relationship that is not healthy for you. You might engage in activities that undermine your values. Unless you check and adjust your attitude, negativity will become self-defeating and self-inhibiting. Here are five examples:

Case Example #1

Rose was a 34-year-old female attorney and successful partner in a large law firm, divorced, with no children. She sought treatment because she was having trouble coping with her failed marriage and dating. Here's her story:

"I guess I was pretty bitter and angry after my husband left. During our marriage I did everything a woman should or could do. I cooked, cleaned and took care of his needs while working. I made love to him even when I was tired. Whatever he wanted I tried my best to give it.

We did not have any noticeable problems and I assumed we were happily married. However, about 5 years into our marriage he began to distance himself. He did not spend much time with me or want to be intimate. When I asked him what was going on he told me that he was falling out of love with me. I was totally surprised and pleaded with him to stay. I asked if we could seek marital therapy and he said no.

My husband was very stubborn and often did not share his emotions. If we had a disagreement he would withdraw. After a while I figured out that I would be better off if I did not pursue him. Unfortunately, he left me.

To this day I do not know why he left, but I eventually moved on with my life. I swore that I would never be hurt again. I date occasionally, but I do not take men seriously. I built myself back up. I am a strong woman. I really don't need a man. I can take care of myself financially. I meet nice guys, but I often chase them away after a few dates. **I don't express emotions frequently or let them know that I am enjoying them.** They tell me that I have an "I don't care attitude." I don't see anything wrong with me. Someday I would like to get married again, but I struggle".

Case Example #2

Pam was a 25-year-old female high school graduate, manager of a fast food restaurant, single, with three children. She was seeking treatment because she was suffering from low self-esteem and having trouble finding a good man that will love and respect her. Here's her story:

"During my childhood, I was physically and sexually abused. When I was twelve years old, my mother left me with one of her male friends who molested me. This happened several more times and I never told anyone for years.

For years I believed that I was worthless and struggled to love any man. I dated guys who always wanted sex. I never thought anything was wrong with it because I like sex. Unfortunately, my children have different fathers. I tried to do right by being with one man, but it did not work out. **I don't try to do the right thing anymore.** Doing the right thing does not get my children fed or pay my bills so I use my body to get money. Caring got me two children and no man. If a man wants to be with me he has to accept me the way I am. I am a survivor and I let men know upfront. I really want to be loved and I know I should not do some of the things I do, but **I don't care anymore**".

Case Example #3

Sara was a 28-year-old high school graduate, stay-at home wife, with two children. She was seeking treatment because she was suffering from burnout that began one year ago. Here's her story:

"During my childhood I had to take care of myself and my siblings. I could not rely on my parents because they were drug addicts. I cooked, cleaned and did what was needed to maintain our household. I grew up believing that I could not trust people. I learned to take care of things by myself.

I married early. Shortly after I married I felt that it was o.k. to ask my husband to help me. He helped whenever I asked and sometimes when I did not, but for some reason I felt like he would eventually let me down, so I stopped asking for help. **I look for the worst in situations and sometimes my attitude can be negative.** I practically cooked, cleaned and raised our children by myself. If I wanted things done, I did it myself. I realize that I need to share my feelings, but I don't have time. I am too busy".

Case Example #4

John was a 40 year-married, active duty military member, with two children. He was seeking treatment because he was feeling depressed due to marital conflict. Here's his story:

"My wife and I have been married for 12 years and are starting to drift apart. She constantly accuses me of not showing affection. I do not have time to come home and address her emotional needs every day. I take care of all the financial issues and make sure that she has everything she needs. **I want to save my marriage, but I do not have time to be bothered with her pettiness.** I am starting to think that she does not care about my career. I told her that I was a career person when we got married. She recently told me that she did not care about my career and that I should spend more time with her. I do not know what to tell her because I have made too much progress to play around with my career. I love her and my kids, but

-------------------Maintain a Positive Attitude-------------------

94

right now I am focused on what is best for me. She will understand in the long run".

Case Example #5

Mike was a 28-year-old male college graduate, with no children. He was seeking treatment because he was having a hard time bonding with women. Here's his story:

"I don't know where to begin. I just do not trust women. My ex-girlfriend cheated on me and I put up with it for a few years before I decided to leave. I want to trust women, but I am afraid of being hurt. I have tried to let my guard down, but it does not work out. In anticipation that I would get hurt, I usually do something to test the female I'm dating. I would make her upset to see what she would do. **I know I play games, but I don't want to get hurt first. Sometimes I care and sometimes I do not.** I have casual relationships, but find ways to end them before they get too serious. Life is about protecting yourself because no one else will. I don't want to be hurt, but I do want to fall in love someday".

Maintain a Positive Attitude

Unfortunately, as a result of bad relationship experiences, some of you find it is difficult to maintain a positive attitude. The inner negative critic tells you to give up on relationships and love. The internal anguish and frustration caused by this thinking makes you behave in a negative way that distances others, thus reinforcing your desire to distance yourself.

Women and men who go through life with negative attitudes are at greater risk of not giving or receiving unconditional love. Learn to replace negative attitudes with positive attitudes:

Negative Attitudes:

- Rude
- Ungrateful

-----------------------Unconditional Love-----------------------

- Judgmental
- Insensitive
- Unsure
- Pessimistic
- Narrow-minded

Positive Attitudes:

- Peaceful
- Polite
- Thankful
- Non-judgmental
- Compassionate
- Confident
- Optimistic
- Open-minded
- Self-controlled

Maintaining a positive attitude is achievable and can help you give and receive unconditional love. To successfully maintain a positive attitude, you must adjust your thinking. Effectively applying the seven strategies below will enable you to have relationships filled with joy and bliss.

1.) **Identify distortions** in your thinking. Faulty thinking is unhealthy for you. Identifying negative attitudes is the first step to maintaining a positive attitude.

_____
_____
_____
_____
_____
_____
_____
_____
_____

2.)   **Counter your inner critic** by challenging the negative inner voice that attacks and judges you and others. Frequent monitoring of your inner critic prevents distortions from manifesting.

_____
_____
_____
_____
_____
_____
_____
_____
_____

3.)   **Identify your strengths** and establish an accurate list of them as well as your resources. Review your list daily to remind yourself of your strengths.

_____
_____
_____
_____
_____
_____
_____
_____
_____

4.)   **Use thought stopping.** When the inner critic attacks aggressively, stop the negative thinking and revisit healthy thoughts.

_____
_____
_____
_____
_____
_____
_____
_____
_____

-----------------------Unconditional Love-----------------------

5.) **Accept yourself and others without passing judgment.** Deal with facts only and eliminate negative emotions.

_____
_____
_____
_____
_____
_____
_____
_____
_____

6.) **Avoid being passive and inflexible.** Express your emotions assertively and be open to feedback and change.

_____
_____
_____
_____
_____
_____
_____
_____
_____

7.) **Reinforce healthy self-talk.** Use positive affirmations to reinforce healthy self-talk. Examples: "I will have a healthy relationship filled with unconditional love; and I will not give up until I achieve the result I desire."

_____
_____
_____
_____
_____
_____
_____
_____
_____

-------------------Maintain a Positive Attitude-------------------

Maintaining and fostering a positive attitude requires you to be flexible in your thinking. It is important to understand alternative viewpoints. It is also important to understand yourself. You are your worst critic. What you feel or tell yourself is not always true or accurate. Looking for the good in yourself and others should become a habit. A habit is a point where desire, knowledge, and skill meet. Take time to learn about your significant other by being active, looking for common ground, not assuming differences in meaning, and looking for and respecting individuality. Be mindful that maintaining a positive attitude toward yourself and your significant other does not guarantee that you will receive unconditional love. However, it will allow you to give it. Hopefully what goes around comes back around. Change your attitude and increase your chance of giving and receiving unconditional love. Remove negativity from your mind and heart. Do not allow a negative attitude to rob you of the unconditional love you deserve!

"The key to giving and receiving unconditional love begins with your attitude"

What kind of attitude do you exhibit daily?
Is your attitude enhancing or destroying your relationship?
How do you plan to change your attitude if it is destroying your relationship?

_____
_____
_____
_____
_____
_____
_____
_____
_____
_____
_____
_____
_____
_____
_____
_____
_____

------------------Maintain a Positive Attitude------------------

8

Strategy #4:

Love without Limits

"Don't Be Afraid To Give Your All"

Loving without limits is the fourth strategy to giving and receiving unconditional love in your relationship. Unconditional love sees no limits, feels no limits and believes no limits. Your heart can and will go wherever you direct it. Direct your heart toward God and reap the benefits of loving without limits. Do you know what it means to love someone without limits?

People go through life feeling deprived of love because they are improperly equipped. Many people are conditioned to believe that love can be earned by doing good deed, conditioned to believe that we should only love those who love us and conditioned to believe that love does not hurt.

Your ability to love yourself and others unconditionally is challenging, because you do not know what true love is. You often look for love in the wrong places. The heart of God and the gospel of Christ is love. Love is compassion, grace, sacrifice, and mercy. Yes, compassion, sacrifice, and mercy! Sometimes you have to be willing to give up someone or something you love to demonstrate compassion for others. God sacrificed His only begotten Son to show us how much He loves us. He continues to show love for you despite your

-----------------------Unconditional Love-----------------------

103

wrongdoing. Loving others, like God loves you, can be difficult, but giving and receiving unconditional love is impossible until you learn to love as He loves. It is easy to fall victim to loving others based on conditions. However, I am delighted that God does not love us based on conditions because we have all fallen short of His glory.

We are cohorts on our journey to reach heaven. Our greatest challenge is loving ourselves and others unconditionally. How can we overcome this challenge? The first step is to love without forcing our rules, requirements, and conditions on others. Let me explain! God loves us so much that He allows us to do as we please. He does not force His love on us or remove it based on our actions. It is true that He has rules for His children and expects us to follow them. But He loves us without limit. He permits us to make mistakes and continues to love us even if He does not approve of our behavior. His compassion for us is immeasurable. He is merciful to those who wrong Him or disobey Him. He does not force us to change. Instead, He provides a firsthand lesson on how to love unconditionally. He teaches us how to love daily and never forsakes us. His love is love without limits. Do you know what this means?

To love unconditionally, you must allow others to exercise their *free will*. Yes! It is your responsibility to hold your significant other accountable; and Yes! it is your responsibility to assertively confront him or her when you feel wronged. But remember, you cannot control other people. Understanding the difference between control and influence will enable you to love unconditionally. **Control** means to master or command. **Influence** is the act or power of producing an effect without obvious application of force or direct exercise of command. As mentioned earlier, God does not force us to love Him, and He does not withhold His love. At this point, you are probably wondering how this applies to you and your relationship.

Love to influence, not to control

One of the major problems that exist in many relationships is withholding love to control others. You have made it known to your wife, husband or significant other that if he or she behaves in a certain way, you will withdraw your love. Is this behavior Godly?

God commands us to love others without limiting their ability or freedom to exercise their *free will*. I realize that this is a difficult task, especially if you have failed to stand up for yourself previously and have been hurt. As a responsible and mature individual, you decide how to interact with others, but keep in mind that aggressive and controlling behavior does not facilitate openness and growth. If you are upset or desire certain behavior, provide your significant other with as much information as possible to make good decisions, but do not force your thoughts or solutions on him or her. Your job is to influence his or her behavior and let him or her know that you will love them unconditionally regardless of what they decide. This is what God does. He is always present and loves you when you are sick or healthy; happy or sad; obedient or disobedient. He loves us enough to give us total freedom. He wants us to love Him by choice, not by force. When you love someone unconditionally, and they know it, all doubt, fear, and anxiety is removed from their heart. I strongly encourage you to apply this principle in your marriage and relationships. Love to influence, not to control.

God instructs us to love others despite their behavior, appearance or flaws. Inflicting pain, holding grudges or hatred against your significant other will never free you to love without limits. Loving unconditionally is God's remedy to nurturing broken hearts and unhealthy relationships. At times you might question your ability to love those who hurt or upset you; but once you let go, all the harsh emotions and turmoil will disappear. Would you like to experience love like this? Do you believe it is humanly possible to love unconditionally?

I hope you answered yes! God created you in His likeness and blessed you with the gift of love. All you must do is apply what is in your heart. Do you believe? Let's explore four strategies you can implement to practice loving others as well as yourself unconditionally.

1. Love like God
2. Understand Love
3. Have Compassion
4. Be Forgiving

Strategy 1: Love like God

God's love is total, says his apostle Paul. It reaches every corner of our experience. It is wide. It covers the breadth of our own experience and reaches out to the whole world. God's love is long - it continues the length of our lives. It is high - it rises to the heights of our celebration and elation. His love is deep – it reaches to the depth of discouragement, despair, and even death (Ephesians 3:17-19).

Strategy 2: Understand Love

Love is not hate; Love is not resentful; Love is not conditional; Love is not pride; Love is not limited; Love is not a gift from man; Love is not to be taken for granted; Love is not restricted to a specific race or gender. Let me be clear, love is God.

Strategy 3: Have Compassion for others

Do you know the difference between sympathy and compassion? Sympathy means to feel sorry for someone, but it does not require you to do anything. Compassion, on the other hand, means to feel sympathetic to another's pain, but it requires action. An individual who is compassionate takes action to relieve others of their suffering. A compassionate person does what is right even in difficult times. When no one else will step up, a compassionate person does. This is what Jesus did for us. A compassionate person does not judge others; instead, he or she helps when warranted. To have a relationship with Jesus and live a Christ-like lifestyle, you must have compassion for others. Compassion fulfills the law of Christ (Galatians 6:2).

Strategy 4: Be Forgiving

Forgiving others is not easy, but God requires you to. If you desire forgiveness, you must be willing to forgive. Refusing to forgive others is a sign of selfishness. God is not selfish, so He expects you to forgive others.

I know it feels unfair to forgive individuals who have emotionally, physically or sexually abused you, neglected you, embarrassed you or belittled you, but forgiveness will enable you to heal. Letting go of anger and hatred is healthy for you and uplifts God's kingdom. Forgiveness is our Godly obligation. Also, forgiveness empowers you to take control over your emotions. As long as you harbor unforgiveness, you are empowering those who hurt you. When you release bitterness, you allow God's forgiveness to pour into your life.

Keep in mind that unforgiveness is a negative emotion that handicaps you. If you walk around holding grudges, you will deprive yourself of God's blessings. Some people will offend you; go home and do not think twice about their behavior. You must let go and move on. Remember that no one is perfect, including you. Each one of us has offended someone, so it is important to forgive others so God can forgive you. Pray for those who hurt you because they are hurting themselves. If it is possible and safe, seek to understand their rage; otherwise remove yourself from the situation and pray for them.

Do not permit anyone to strip you of your gift of love. God created you out of love so that you can love yourself and others. Don't be afraid to love yourself and others unconditionally. The benefits will be great depending on your attitude. Nelson Mandela glorified the importance of loving yourself and living without fear by stating, "As we let our light shine, we unconsciously give other people permission to do the same. As we're liberated from our own fear, our presence automatically liberates others."

"Apply Strategies"

Identify an individual that you are having difficulty loving unconditionally and apply the strategies to recondition your heart.

Strategy 1: Love like God

_____
_____
_____
_____
_____
_____

Strategy 2: Understand Love

_____
_____
_____
_____
_____
_____

Strategy 3: Have Compassion

_____
_____
_____
_____
_____
_____

Strategy 4: Be Merciful – Forgive

_____
_____
_____
_____
_____
_____

--------------------Love without Limits--------------------

"Unconditional Love sees no limits, feels no limits and accepts no limits"

What does loving without limits mean to you? Are you capable of loving without limits? Why or Why not?

Do you understand what it means to love someone without limits?

_____
_____
_____
_____
_____
_____
_____
_____
_____
_____
_____
_____
_____
_____
_____
_____
_____
_____
_____

-----------------------Unconditional Love-----------------------

PART THREE

SUSTAINING UNCONDITIONAL LOVE

9

Seek Marital and Spiritual Guidance

"Become a Whole Person"

Many of us go through life trying to figure out how to develop and sustain unconditional love in our relationships, but unfortunately lack the basic skills that are vital to addressing and resolving our shortcomings. How many individuals do you know or have met who seem to be grounded spiritually, but appear to lack effective communication and interpersonal skills? How many individuals do you know or have met who seem to have effective communication and interpersonal skills, but lack spiritual maturity?

I work with, fellowship with and interact with individuals who fall into either category daily, and have learned that they are not capable of giving or receiving unconditional love in their relationships because they are not "whole". Some of them are skilled in applying basic psychology and self-help techniques, but lack spiritual maturity. Others are skilled in applying scripture and Christian principles, but lack day-to-day self-help coping skills. A "whole" person is equipped with practical and spiritual knowledge and lives a balanced lifestyle by applying both in his or her daily interactions. However, achieving wholeness is not an easy task because individuals who seek marital counseling are sometimes perceived to be "crazy" or "unstable". Such negative stereotypes reinforce couples' resistance to seeking help even when they need it.

A "whole" person is equipped with practical and spiritual knowledge and lives a balanced lifestyle by applying both in his or her daily interactions.

In my early years as a therapist I did not understand why individuals were willing to seek therapy to save relationships that appeared to be destructive and unhealthy. Like others, I did not understand the point. However, after years of listening to hundreds of couples, I began to understand what it means to fight for something you want. While others may view therapy seekers negatively, I view them as role models. They recognize that their relationships are in trouble and seek help. This behavior is far from being "crazy". In actuality, individuals who realize that their relationships are troubled but continue to do the same thing daily without seeking help might better fit the definition of "crazy".

I have found that individuals who combine professional counseling and spiritual guidance are more capable of developing healthy coping skills and approach relationship conflict with balanced perspectives. Through a combination of marital and spiritual guidance, individuals can acquire knowledge that will enhance their ability to give and receive unconditional love in their relationships. Let's review a session I had with a client who was spiritually grounded, but continued to experience difficulty in her relationship:

Me: How are things going between your husband and you?

Jane: We continue to argue over simple things and end up frustrating each other. We pray for each other and together. We have talked to the pastor several times and received some helpful guidance. Things get better for a while, but we continue to communicate ineffectively.

Me: What contributes to or causes conflict in your opinion?

Jane: I believe we have different communication styles. Growing up I was told that God would fulfill all my needs. I embraced my spiritual guidance and attempted to apply what I learned daily. My parents did not verbally express their emotions openly and when they had disagreements they prayed and moved on. Occasionally I would hear both of them blaming each other for conflicts that aroused. Neither of my parents took responsibility for their contribution to the conflict. Conversations typically started off with "You made me". This pattern of communication was common in my household. My parents did not appear to communicate very well, but remained committed to each other through their spiritual maturity. They definitely loved each other, but could not communicate without arguing. I believe I adopted my parents' style of communication. I have a tendency to blame my husband for how I feel. My husband on the other hand, does not express his feelings. He rarely gets upset, but when he does, he blames me for making him feel that way. We start conversations similar to the way my parents start, "You made me". I respect my husband as the Bible instructs me to, but I am starting to lose respect for him. I pray and ask forgiveness when I am angry and bitter, but I don't know if I love him. I do not understand how a relationship that is filled with so much spirituality continues to decline. If it was not for my faith, I would have probably left by now.

Me: So it sounds like you both attack and accuse each other for feeling a certain way and this causes communication to come to a halt. Instead of listening, both of you are defending why you feel the way you do.

Jane: You are correct! How can we communicate more effectively? I want to save my marriage and stop fighting so much.

Me: Try using "I messages". "I messages" are used to avoid blaming others for how you feel. "I messages" facilitate healthy communication by encouraging each of you to take responsibility for your emotions. Instead of saying, "You made me mad because you did do what you said you would do", say "I feel mad because you did not do what you said you would do".

Jane: What is the difference?

Me: First, whenever you start a conversation with "You", an individuals' natural response is to defend themselves which decreases the likelihood that they will comprehend anything that is being said to them. As you are talking to them they are thinking about their defensive response ("I did not make you mad because"). Placing blame on others causes individuals to become defensive. Second, no one can make you feel anything that you do not want to feel. You are responsible for your emotions and have the power to control them. Do you understand why it is important to use "I messages"?

Jane: Yes! I wish I had learned this skill sooner. I definitely know the importance of treating others as I would like to be treated. My spirituality helps me in so many ways, but I often feel that I lack the skills to deal with my marriage on a daily basis. However, application of this simple communication technique will make a world of difference in my relationship.

Acquiring knowledge through marital guidance and then combining it with spiritual guidance will position you to become the whole person that God wants you to be. You must learn how to navigate in the world without being part of it. Every person you encounter will not be spiritually savvy or have excellent inter-personal or communication skills so it is important to live a balanced life.

I believe that it is important to seek marital guidance to learn effective coping skills and receive spiritual guidance to learn and understand what God instructs you to do to sustain unconditional love in your relationship. Think of marital guidance as the mechanism that

-------------Seek Marital and Spiritual Guidance------------

provides the coping skills you need to apply the knowledge you learn through spiritual guidance. Relationships are difficult to sustain without God's presence and without effective interpersonal and communication skills.

Until you learn to achieve balance, you will continue to experience unnecessary hardships in your relationships. You will not always understand everything that happens in your relationship and at times will struggle to sustain it, but the *Word* teaches you to: "Trust in the LORD with all thine heart; and lean not unto thine own understanding. In all thy ways acknowledge Him, and He shall direct thy paths" (Proverbs 3:5-6). Work to nurture your spirituality, but remember to develop effective coping skills along the way.

People navigate through life and relationships by using their "common sense" instead of developing effective coping skills. The sole use of common sense is not very effective in my opinion because common sense is really not so common. Individuals typically do what is common to them. For example, as a young boy I treated girls disrespectfully because I observed that behavior daily. I knew my behavior was wrong, but behaved that way because it was "common" to me -everybody else did it. Individual life experiences develop common sense so be mindful of others' experiences before you make assumptions that they are using "common sense". No two people are the same. With this in mind, do not solely rely on what is common to you, especially if it is not working. Seek guidance.

To sustain unconditional love in your relationship, start by restoring or enhancing your spiritual relationship with God. Through God all things are possible. As you connect with God, you become free from the shackles of anger, frustration and resentment. This does not mean that you will not continue to experience difficulty because others are liberated to use their *free will* as they see fit. However, it does means that you will be better equipped to cope with it. If you are spiritually grounded, but continue to have difficulty sustaining unconditional love in your relationship, seek premarital or marital guidance. As stated earlier, relationships require work so after you pray, attend church and consult with your pastor, be prepared to learn and apply effective communication, stress and anger management skills that you can use daily to sustain unconditional love. If you maximize your options, I guarantee that sustaining unconditional love will come with minimum distress. You should always strive to enhance your spiritual, emotional, intellectual and physical well-being. This is the true meaning of becoming a whole person.

"A whole person is equipped with practical and spiritual knowledge and applies both in his or her daily interactions"

Do you feel that it is necessary to possess practical and spiritual knowledge to have a healthy relationship?
Why or Why not?

_____
_____
_____
_____
_____
_____
_____
_____
_____
_____
_____
_____
_____
_____
_____
_____
_____
_____
_____
_____

10

Practice Loving Self Unconditionally

"Love from within illuminates outwardly"

The ability to love yourself unconditionally can be difficult, especially if you have experienced hardships such as sexual, physical or emotional abuse. However, remember that your life experiences do not define who you are. Unfortunately, bad things happen to good people. Your ability to cope with hardships defines your true character. Do not fall victim to loving yourself based on conditions. Love yourself regardless of your appearance, background, economic, social or financial status. I realize that this is a complex task because people can be very judgmental. Remember that God did not create perfect people. Some individuals may appear to have it all together. They might even appear to be perfect, but Jesus was the only perfect human that ever walked this earth. Do not live your life stressing over being perfect. Instead, live it doing the best you can. Challenge yourself to objectively eliminate emotions, expectations and attitudes that make you feel unlovable.

You are special because you share the image of God. When you are feeling down remember that life is a gift from God. Need I say more? Your ability to love yourself unconditionally depends on what you tell yourself, how you treat yourself, and how you interpret your world. If loving yourself requires others to approve of you, you might find yourself feeling frustrated, helpless and powerless. Seeking the approval of others can lead to burnout and demoralizing behavior. Work at loving yourself and improving your self-esteem. People with high self-esteem view themselves positively. They often feel good about themselves and appreciate their own worth.

Now that I have your undivided attention and you are inspired to love yourself unconditionally let's look at empowering self-love techniques you can implement to improve your self-esteem which will help you learn to love yourself unconditionally.

1. Love God First
2. Set your own personal standards
3. Use encouraging, positive language
4. Identify your strengths
5. Eliminate self-defeating/irrational thinking
6. Do away with perfectionist thinking

Self-Love Technique 1: Love God First

God created you to love Him, but many of you look for love in all the wrong places. True happiness and unconditional love for yourself and others will not occur until you learn to love God first. God is love and He loves you unconditionally. You are His child. Do not distance yourself from your Father when evil things happen to you or your loved ones. Remember that God gave us all the gift of *free will*. Be mindful that your attempt to walk righteously does not exclude you from experiencing bad things. Others have *free will* too and when they choose to be of the world instead of God, evil things will happen. Evil is present where God is absent. Keep God in your heart, mind and soul and loving yourself unconditionally will come easily. Unconditional love for self and others is only possible by reordering your love by putting God first.

Therefore if any man be in Christ, he is a new creature: old things are passed away; behold, all things are become new (II Corinthians 5:17).

--------------Practice Loving Self Unconditionally------------

But seek ye first the kingdom of God, and his righteousness; and all these things shall be added unto you (Matthew 6:33)

Self-Love Technique 2: Set your own personal standards

To start loving yourself, simply set your own standards. Do not live your life according to how others view you. Avoid comparing yourself to others and using belittling words such as stupid, unattractive, powerless, worthless, and shallow to describe yourself. Pay close attention to how you define and describe yourself. Stop negative self-attacks.

Self-Love Technique 3: Use encouraging, positive language

"The tongue of the wise useth knowledge aright: but the mouth of fools poureth out foolishness" (Proverbs 15:2). When you talk to yourself and to others about yourself, use positive and inspiring statements. Such statements are called affirmations. Effective use of affirmations can help you change problem areas in your life. Identify a problem in your life and set a goal. Use affirmations that describe that goal. Some examples of affirmations include:

- I am lovable and worthy of being happy in my life and in my relationship.
- I am intelligent and really feel good about it.
- I can cope with life challenges in a healthy manner.
- I handle disappointment calmly and reasonably.
- I have a right to make mistakes.
- I can let go of my need to control others.
- I cope with despair and pain rationally.

Learn to write affirmations that use present tense, define what you want, what already exists, and what makes you feel good. Use specific, personal, action-oriented words that are short and to the point. Develop a list of affirmations that are meaningful to you and speak them daily. If your affirmations do not produce your desired outcome, write new ones. Remember that what you say to yourself and to others about yourself is often stored subconsciously in your mind and in theirs.

Self-Love Technique 4: Identify your strengths

Conduct an accurate and honest self-assessment. Develop a valid list of your strengths and assets. If you suffer from low self-esteem it probably did not occur overnight. Remind yourself of your strengths daily and take an inventory. Use that inventory to help you identify blessings, accomplishments and goals you have achieved that support your dreams and ambitions.

Self-Love Technique 5: Eliminate self-defeating/irrational beliefs

Question your old beliefs and replace them with new ones. Too often you hold on to the unhealthy beliefs with which you grew up. Some of your beliefs are healthy and some are not. If the following beliefs are in your mind, eliminate them:

- If I ask for help, I'll look weak.
- If people knew the real me, they would dislike me.
- If I fail, I'm a loser.
- I should never feel hopeless, helpless, powerless, tired or depressed.
- I am nothing unless I am loved.
- I should be totally self-sufficient and independent.
- I have to be right all the time or I won't be respected.
- I am the only one who understands me and can solve my problems.
- If I try hard enough, I can succeed at anything and everything.
- Some people are better than others.
- I need to be smart, rich, powerful and attractive to be happy.
- Life isn't fair, and I can't handle it.
- It reflects poorly on me if my relationship or marriage does not work.

--------------Practice Loving Self Unconditionally------------

Eliminating self-defeating/irrational thinking can help you see and experience life more objectively. Your mind is powerful and, if used inappropriately, it can cause you to self-destruct. Examine your beliefs and ask yourself several questions. What evidence do I have to support my beliefs? Are my beliefs beneficial or healthy? Do they make me feel good or bad? After carefully reviewing your beliefs, you might find that you need to eliminate some of them and replace them with new ones. Don't be discouraged or beat yourself up during this process. Changing your way of thinking can be a complex process. After all, you did not become the person you are in an instant.

Self-Love Technique 6: Do away with perfectionist thinking

While it is important to look, feel and do well, remember that you are not and will never be perfect. Striving for perfection can lead to unrealistic expectations of yourself and others. Do your best to accept yourself while enhancing your performance and having fun. Life is too short to live it thinking you must do everything perfectly or not at all. Perfectionist thinking can lead to hard work and no pleasure. You cannot do it all. Enjoy life, yourself and others and ask for help when you need it.

Improving your self-esteem and loving yourself unconditionally can be one of the most rewarding things you will ever do. Do not let others rob you of your gift of life. God created you out of love so you can love yourself and others. Don't be afraid to love yourself. The benefits can be profound.

To love yourself unconditionally, practice the self-love techniques listed above daily, share your commitment with others and use the following quotation for inspiration:

"The ultimate lesson all of us have to learn is unconditional love, which includes not only others but ourselves as well."

—*Elisabeth Kubler-Ross*

-----------------------Unconditional Love-----------------------

Apply Techniques

Identify a problem or issue you are experiencing that negatively influences how you view yourself and apply the self-love techniques to improve your self-esteem and increase your ability to love yourself unconditionally.

Self-Love Technique 1: Love God first

_____
_____
_____
_____
_____
_____
_____

Self-Love Technique 2: Set your own personal standards

_____
_____
_____
_____
_____
_____
_____

Self-Love Technique 3: Use encouraging, positive language

_____
_____
_____
_____
_____
_____
_____

-------------Practice Loving Self Unconditionally------------

Self-Love Technique 4: Identify Your Strengths

_____

_____

_____

_____

_____

_____

_____

Self-Love Technique 5: Eliminate self-defeating/irrational beliefs

_____

_____

_____

_____

_____

_____

_____

Self-Love Technique 6: Do away with perfectionist thinking

_____

_____

_____

_____

_____

_____

_____

"Love for self is healthy for your soul and relationship"

Is it possible to love others if you do not love yourself?
Why or Why not?

Why is it important to love yourself unconditionally?

_____
_____
_____
_____
_____
_____
_____
_____
_____
_____
_____
_____
_____
_____
_____
_____
_____
_____
_____

--------------Practice Loving Self Unconditionally------------

11

99 Relationship Sustainment Strategies

"But wilt thou know, O vain man, that faith without works is dead" James 2:20

Work is notable and demonstrates faith in God. We serve a God that cares about our relationships as well as our spiritual needs. Our relational needs are met in part by the work we do. Anything in life worth having is gained through diligence and work. You do not have to walk away from a relationship if you are willing to work (99% of the time). No relationship comes without hardships, trials and tribulation, but relationships without work are typically consumed by those hardships, trials and tribulation. If you desire to make your relationship last forever, embrace and implement the 99 Relationship Sustainment Strategies listed below.

Relationship Sustainment Strategy #1

Talk with your significant other; not at him or her. Respect is not optional in healthy relationships.

Write it here:

_____
_____
_____
_____
_____
_____
_____
_____
_____

Relationship Sustainment Strategy #2

Show interest in things that are important to your significant other.

Write it here:

_____
_____
_____
_____
_____
_____
_____
_____
_____

Relationship Sustainment Strategy #3

Develop and engage in activities that you both enjoy (cooking, working-out, etc.)

Write it here:

_____
_____
_____
_____
_____
_____
_____
_____
_____

Relationship Sustainment Strategy #4

Schedule couple time outside of family time. Focusing attention on your significant other demonstrates that you care about his or her needs.

Write it here:

_____
_____
_____
_____
_____
_____
_____
_____
_____

-----------------------Unconditional Love-----------------------

Relationship Sustainment Strategy #5

Be creative. Do not stick to the same routine. Try new things sexually, physically and emotionally.

Write it here:

_____
_____
_____
_____
_____
_____
_____
_____
_____

Relationship Sustainment Strategy #6

Validate emotions. The root cause of most relational conflict is caused by invalidation of emotions. How a person feels is real to him or her. The quickest way to resolve emotional distress is to recognize and respect it. This does not mean that you will always understand or agree with your significant other's emotions; simply validate them.

Write it here:

_____
_____
_____
_____
_____
_____
_____
_____
_____

Relationship Sustainment Strategy #7

Learn to recognize and address your significant other's perceptions. A person's perception is his or her reality. Do not argue about perceptions, instead recognize them and work to resolve incorrect perceptions.

Write it here:

_____
_____
_____
_____
_____
_____
_____
_____
_____

Relationship Sustainment Strategy #8

Schedule positive reflection time; identify five things you really love about your significant other and spend time reflecting on them.

Write it here:

_____
_____
_____
_____
_____
_____
_____
_____
_____

Relationship Sustainment Strategy #9

Attend a relationship enhancement seminar together and develop a plan to implement what you learned. Team work helps individuals feel that their opinion matters and encourages action due to mutual buy in.

Write it here:

_____
_____
_____
_____
_____
_____
_____
_____

Relationship Sustainment Strategy #10

Avoid emotional and physical abuse. Degrading, belittling or making your significant other feel powerless or worthless is counter-productive to having a healthy relationship. Name calling and insults are abusive tactics that block giving and receiving unconditional love. True love cannot be forced and it does not hurt.

Write it here:

_____
_____
_____
_____
_____
_____
_____
_____

Relationship Sustainment Strategy #11

Respect the need for individual time. There are three components in every relationship: you, me and us. Remember that your significant other had a life before you. One of the biggest challenges for couples is to learn that each person must have time to address personal needs.

Write it here:

_____
_____
_____
_____
_____
_____
_____
_____

Relationship Sustainment Strategy #12

Spend quality time with your significant other. Quantity is not the same as quality. Existing in the same house equates to quantity time, but does not necessarily equate to quality. Meaningful interactions and conversations fall in the realm of quality time.

Write it here:

_____
_____
_____
_____
_____
_____
_____

Relationship Sustainment Strategy #13

Strive to identify with your significant other emotionally, physically and spiritually. Relationships blossom when all three are in harmony.

Write it here:

_____
_____
_____
_____
_____
_____
_____
_____

Relationship Sustainment Strategy #14

Support your significant other's educational, professional and personal goals. Every desire or idea is worth discussing. Hear him or her out before you make a decision or pass judgment. Demonstrate patience, respect and common courtesy. The latter behaviors will enable your significant other to speak freely to you without fear or hesitation.

Write it here:

_____
_____
_____
_____
_____
_____
_____
_____

Relationship Sustainment Strategy #15

Develop and maintain a trusting relationship. Discontinue behaviors that cause your significant other to question your trustworthiness. If there is a significant amount of distress associated with certain actions; simply discontinue them. For example, speaking to or meeting with an old "flame".

Write it here:

_____
_____
_____
_____
_____
_____
_____
_____
_____

Relationship Sustainment Strategy #16

Interact with friends and family members who support your relationship and have positive things to contribute. Remember misery loves miserable company.

Write it here:

_____
_____
_____
_____
_____
_____
_____
_____
_____

----------------------Unconditional Love----------------------

Relationship Sustainment Strategy #17

Be responsible for your actions and words. Remember that no one is responsible for you, but you. Your significant other can contribute to your emotional state, but cannot cause or determine it.

Write it here:

_____
_____
_____
_____
_____
_____
_____
_____
_____

Relationship Sustainment Strategy #18

Learn to agree to disagree. Conflict is not bad unless you cope with it ineffectively. You can disagree with your significant other without being disrespectful.

Write it here:

_____
_____
_____
_____
_____
_____
_____
_____
_____

Relationship Sustainment Strategy #19

Build on the friendship you initially established with your significant other when you first courted.

Write it here:

_____
_____
_____
_____
_____
_____
_____
_____
_____

Relationship Sustainment Strategy #20

Apologize with words. Gifts are nice, but do not have the same effect as kind words. Words of kindness please the heart and soul.

Write it here:

_____
_____
_____
_____
_____
_____
_____
_____
_____

Relationship Sustainment Strategy #21

Eliminate prideful attitudes. Too much pride is unhealthy and can prevent you from humbling yourself. Arrogant individuals see the value in themselves. In contrast, humble individuals see the value in themselves and others.

Write it here:

_____
_____
_____
_____
_____
_____
_____
_____
_____

Relationship Sustainment Strategy #22

Share responsibility for making decisions in your relationship. Empower your significant other to actively participate in decisions that affect the both of you.

Write it here:

_____
_____
_____
_____
_____
_____
_____
_____
_____

Relationship Sustainment Strategy #23

Divide household chores and parental responsibilities. Sharing of tasks can potentially prevent burnout. Individuals who are suffering from burnout or physical and emotional exhaustion are more likely to function in an unproductive and unhealthy manner. Give your significant other some help and benefit from the energy of your rejuvenated spouse.

Write it here:

_____
_____
_____
_____
_____
_____
_____
_____

Relationship Sustainment Strategy #24

Let your significant other know that you are proud to be with him or her. Demonstrate your fondness through your actions. Do little things to show them how happy you are to be with them.

Write it here:

_____
_____
_____
_____
_____
_____
_____
_____

Relationship Sustainment Strategy #25

Discuss perceived or actual changes in attitudes or behavior. Your significant other may or may not be aware of his or her attitude or behavior. Never assume anything. Assumptions contribute to poor communication.

Write it here:

_____
_____
_____
_____
_____
_____
_____
_____
_____

Relationship Sustainment Strategy #26

Do not diminish your significant other's worth or value. Each person has something valuable to contribute to the relationship.

Write it here:

_____
_____
_____
_____
_____
_____
_____
_____
_____

Relationship Sustainment Strategy #27

Focus on and address behavior not, character flaws. Attacking character flaws contributes to feelings of anger and frustration. Individuals can work on their behavior more easily than character flaws.

Write it here:

_____
_____
_____
_____
_____
_____
_____
_____
_____

Relationship Sustainment Strategy #28

Do not constantly remind your significant other of his or her imperfections. If you desire change, build up their spirit by making positive statements.

Write it here:

_____
_____
_____
_____
_____
_____
_____
_____
_____

-----------------------Unconditional Love-----------------------

Relationship Sustainment Strategy #29

Demonstrate willingness to stay through the good and bad. Let your significant other know that you are committed to the relationship. Cry and laugh with him or her. Stand by his or her side when faced with adversity.

Write it here:

_____
_____
_____
_____
_____
_____
_____
_____
_____

Relationship Sustainment Strategy #30

Do not allocate your affection based on your significant other's behavior or mood. Love him or her when they are happy, sad, angry or depressed.

Write it here:

_____
_____
_____
_____
_____
_____
_____
_____
_____

Relationship Sustainment Strategy #31

Provide constructive advice or suggestions to your significant other. If you do not have something constructive to say, do not say anything at all.

Write it here:

_____
_____
_____
_____
_____
_____
_____
_____
_____

Relationship Sustainment Strategy #32

Minimize intellectualization of stressors in your relationship. Intellectualizing does not allow you to cope with or address the emotional distress you or your significant other experience. Address underlying emotional stressors in order to get to the source of your or your significant other's discomfort.

Write it here:

_____
_____
_____
_____
_____
_____
_____
_____
_____

-----------------------Unconditional Love-----------------------

Relationship Sustainment Strategy #33

Try not to deny your significant other sexual pleasure. While sexual frustration is not the primary reason for extra-marital affairs, it can contribute to infidelity if emotional frustrations are also present. Emotional detachment combined with physical detachment is not good for relationships. Be mindful that some individuals express their love by means of physical and sexual affection.

Write it here:

_____

_____

_____

_____

_____

_____

_____

_____

Relationship Sustainment Strategy #34

Resolve anger and resentment toward your significant other. Built up and unresolved anger and resentment can penetrate every aspect of your relationship. Seek counseling if you cannot resolve these issues.

Write it here:

_____

_____

_____

_____

_____

_____

_____

_____

Relationship Sustainment Strategy #35

Never command, direct or order your significant other to do anything. Ask him or her politely and allow him or her sufficient time to respond to your request. Be as specific as possible about your request, but not demanding.

Write it here:

_____
_____
_____
_____
_____
_____
_____
_____
_____

Relationship Sustainment Strategy #36

Offer solutions to problems instead of nagging without providing viable options.

Write it here:

_____
_____
_____
_____
_____
_____
_____
_____
_____

Relationship Sustainment Strategy #37

Avoid withdrawing, diverting or humoring in order to circumvent emotional discomfort. Learn to face adversity head on, instead of allowing it to resurface later.

Write it here:

_____
_____
_____
_____
_____
_____
_____
_____
_____

Relationship Sustainment Strategy #38

Don't complain about everything your significant other does. Learn to address what is affecting you significantly and be willing to compromise to get your needs met.

Write it here:

_____
_____
_____
_____
_____
_____
_____
_____
_____

Relationship Sustainment Strategy #39

Develop habits that will nurture your relationship and allow it to grow (Think positive, remain calm, be flexible, etc.).

Write it here:

_____
_____
_____
_____
_____
_____
_____
_____
_____

Relationship Sustainment Strategy #40

Don't compare your relationship to other people's relationships. Your relationship with your significant other is unique. Your circumstances might mirror others, but no two couples have exactly the same problems or coping skills. Identify the strengths and weaknesses in your relationship and use these strengths to address your weaknesses.

Write it here:

_____
_____
_____
_____
_____
_____
_____
_____
_____

-----------------------Unconditional Love-----------------------

Relationship Sustainment Strategy #41

Be supportive of each other's efforts regarding childrearing. Frustration surrounding appropriate childrearing can cause relational conflict. Be consistent and reinforce each other's efforts. Do not rely solely on your childhood experience, especially if it differs considerably from your significant other. Eradicate conflict in childrearing practices by working as a team.

Write it here:

_____
_____
_____
_____
_____
_____
_____
_____
_____

Relationship Sustainment Strategy #42

Do as you say and keep your promises. This is the quickest way to establish and maintain trust with your significant other.

Write it here:

_____
_____
_____
_____
_____
_____
_____
_____
_____

Relationship Sustainment Strategy #43

Remember that actions speak louder than words. Your significant other will pay closer attention to what you do than what you say.

Write it here:

_____
_____
_____
_____
_____
_____
_____
_____
_____

Relationship Sustainment Strategy #44

Help your significant other identify shortcomings and work with him or her to correct them.

Write it here:

_____
_____
_____
_____
_____
_____
_____
_____
_____

-----------------------Unconditional Love-----------------------

Relationship Sustainment Strategy #45

Seek to understand and address your problems before you attempt to tackle your significant other's problems. Exhibit the behavior you desire in return and hopefully you will influence your significant other.

Write it here:

_____
_____
_____
_____
_____
_____
_____
_____
_____

Relationship Sustainment Strategy #46

Do not expect your significant other to cope with life problems the way you do. What affects you may not affect your significant other in the same manner. Allow for and encourage personal exploration and coping.

Write it here:

_____
_____
_____
_____
_____
_____
_____
_____
_____

Relationship Sustainment Strategy #47

Increase your awareness of relationship stressors and work to prevent them before they become unmanageable.

Write it here:

_____
_____
_____
_____
_____
_____
_____
_____
_____

Relationship Sustainment Strategy #48

Avoid making lifestyle, financial or other significant changes that affect your significant other without his or her approval.

Write it here:

_____
_____
_____
_____
_____
_____
_____
_____
_____

Relationship Sustainment Strategy #49

Identify and change self-preserving behaviors that are not good for the relationship. For example, you should consider getting rid of your individual bank account if your significant other has expressed disapproval and closed his or her.

Write it here:

_____
_____
_____
_____
_____
_____
_____
_____
_____

Relationship Sustainment Strategy #50

Do away with your need to be in control of yourself or your significant other all the time. This is stress provoking and will cause your relationship to suffer. Learn to relax and take the back seat occasionally. Demonstrate trust in your significant other.

Write it here:

_____
_____
_____
_____
_____
_____
_____
_____
_____

Relationship Sustainment Strategy #51

Do not take out your occupational and job related frustrations on your significant other. Find means to cope with your frustration instead of unloading on your significant other.

Write it here:

_____
_____
_____
_____
_____
_____
_____
_____
_____

Relationship Sustainment Strategy #52

Get rid of perfectionist attitudes and praise your significant other for doing his or her best.

Write it here:

_____
_____
_____
_____
_____
_____
_____
_____
_____

-----------------------Unconditional Love-----------------------

Relationship Sustainment Strategy #53

Be patient and find out how to control your immediate need for satisfaction. Patience is a virtue.

Write it here:

_____
_____
_____
_____
_____
_____
_____
_____
_____

Relationship Sustainment Strategy #54

Utilize time-outs before discussions get heated or become unproductive. Schedule time to address the issues later and follow through.

Write it here:

_____
_____
_____
_____
_____
_____
_____
_____
_____

Relationship Sustainment Strategy #55

Do not take personal responsibility for the actions of your significant other. Accountability is needed to facilitate growth in your relationship.

Write it here:

_____
_____
_____
_____
_____
_____
_____
_____

Relationship Sustainment Strategy #56

Absolutely do not engage in important or sensitive conversations if you or your significant other has consumed alcohol or any other mood altering substances. Alcohol and other substances lower self-consciousness and cause people say and do things that they regret later.

Write it here:

_____
_____
_____
_____
_____
_____
_____
_____

-----------------------Unconditional Love-----------------------

Relationship Sustainment Strategy #57

Work off some of your relational frustration or stress with physical exercise. Exercise is good for your physical and emotional health. It reduces the level of stress in your body. Taking care of yourself can equip you to handle relational stress more effectively.

Write it here:

_____
_____
_____
_____
_____
_____
_____
_____
_____

Relationship Sustainment Strategy #58

Think of relational stress as a challenge to be conquered. Equip yourself with healthy coping tools and prepare for battle. If you believe you can win, you will. However, don't forget you win together.

Write it here:

_____
_____
_____
_____
_____
_____
_____
_____

Relationship Sustainment Strategy #59

Follow the guidance of knowledgeable, objective and unbiased professionals. Family and friends are a great source of support, but they frequently struggle to be objective. Sometimes you need to hear what is good for you not what you want to hear.

Write it here:

_____
_____
_____
_____
_____
_____
_____
_____
_____

Relationship Sustainment Strategy #60

Think before you take action. Never respond in the heat of the moment.

Write it here:

_____
_____
_____
_____
_____
_____
_____
_____
_____

-----------------------Unconditional Love-----------------------

Relationship Sustainment Strategy #61

Establish a spiritual relationship with God. Individuals who believe in a Higher Power typically attempt to cope with relational stress in a positive manner. Prayer and meditation can reduce personal stress and enhance your relationship.

Write it here:

_____
_____
_____
_____
_____
_____
_____
_____
_____

Relationship Sustainment Strategy #62

Develop a relaxation plan for you and your significant other that involves deep breathing, progressive muscle relaxation and guided imagery. Relaxation helps neutralize stress chemicals in your body.

Write it here:

_____
_____
_____
_____
_____
_____
_____
_____

Relationship Sustainment Strategy #63

Avoid mind games. You cannot have a healthy relationship with your significant other if you take everything lightly or turn everything into a joke.

Write it here:

_____
_____
_____
_____
_____
_____
_____
_____
_____

Relationship Sustainment Strategy #64

Acknowledge and vocalize your insecurities. Do not act like you are strong all the time or do not care when you really do. Insecurities let your significant other know that you have vulnerabilities and will occasionally need reassurance. Arrogance will destroy you and your relationship.

Write it here:

_____
_____
_____
_____
_____
_____
_____
_____
_____

-----------------------Unconditional Love-----------------------

Relationship Sustainment Strategy #65

Pray daily and seek spiritual guidance if your relationship becomes intensely stressful for you and your significant other.

Write it here:

_____
_____
_____
_____
_____
_____
_____
_____
_____

Relationship Sustainment Strategy #66

Seek professional help if you or your significant other experience frequent loss of emotional control or begin to withdrawal from each other.

Write it here:

_____
_____
_____
_____
_____
_____
_____
_____
_____

Relationship Sustainment Strategy #67

Do not rehash unpleasant events. What is done is done. Move forward or move on.

Write it here:

_____
_____
_____
_____
_____
_____
_____
_____
_____

Relationship Sustainment Strategy #68

Exercise your *free will* for the betterment of your relationship. Always chose to do what is best for you and your significant other if possible.

Write it here:

_____
_____
_____
_____
_____
_____
_____
_____
_____

Relationship Sustainment Strategy #69

Minimize or eliminate the use of "I" talk from your relationship dialogues and incorporate some "we" talk.

Write it here:

_____
_____
_____
_____
_____
_____
_____
_____
_____

Relationship Sustainment Strategy #70

Strive to give the best in your relationship by viewing each day as a new opportunity to do something positive that will elevate your relationship to a new level.

Write it here:

_____
_____
_____
_____
_____
_____
_____
_____
_____

Relationship Sustainment Strategy #71

Use money to enhance your relationship, not control it. Money is not the root of all evil; people are. Money can buy a lot of things, but it cannot buy unconditional love.

Write it here:

_____
_____
_____
_____
_____
_____
_____
_____
_____

Relationship Sustainment Strategy #72

Apply the Golden rule in your relationship. Do unto your significant other as you would have him or her do unto you.

Write it here:

_____
_____
_____
_____
_____
_____
_____
_____
_____

-----------------------Unconditional Love-----------------------

Relationship Sustainment Strategy #73

Use positive affirmations to help you cope with difficult situations in your relationship. For example, "I am capable of dealing with anything I put my mind to".

Write it here:

_____
_____
_____
_____
_____
_____
_____
_____
_____

Relationship Sustainment Strategy #74

Set attainable relationship goals such as reducing arguments or conflicts from five times a week to three times a week. Measurable and realistic goals are manageable and can lead to increased relationship satisfaction when accomplished.

Write it here:

_____
_____
_____
_____
_____
_____
_____
_____
_____

Relationship Sustainment Strategy #75

Expand your negotiation and compromise skills by attending assertiveness training. Learn to express your interests, preferences and expectations in a non-aggressive manner. Assertiveness can facilitate positive communication by reducing defensiveness in your significant other.

Write it here:

_____
_____
_____
_____
_____
_____
_____
_____
_____

Relationship Sustainment Strategy #76

Develop and use behavioral contracts in your relationship. You and your spouse should agree to specific behavioral changes and reward each other for meeting specified goals.

Write it here:

_____
_____
_____
_____
_____
_____
_____
_____
_____

-----------------------Unconditional Love-----------------------

Relationship Sustainment Strategy #77

Never accuse your significant other of wrong doing without evidence. Have evidence to back your claim. No one likes to be falsely accused.

Write it here:

_____
_____
_____
_____
_____
_____
_____
_____
_____

Relationship Sustainment Strategy #78

Be adventurous. Engage in a team building activity that requires you and your significant other to depend on each other. Such an experience can enhance or restore trust and nurture the deep love you have for each other.

Write it here:

_____
_____
_____
_____
_____
_____
_____
_____
_____

Relationship Sustainment Strategy #79

Demonstrate faith in your significant other. When things are not going well in your relationship or life in general, let your significant other know that you believe in him or her. Boost his or her confidence and promote a can do attitude.

Write it here:

_____
_____
_____
_____
_____
_____
_____
_____
_____

Relationship Sustainment Strategy #80

Never treat your significant other nonchalantly. Do not deny him or her, the compassion and love you have in your heart.

Write it here:

_____
_____
_____
_____
_____
_____
_____
_____
_____

Relationship Sustainment Strategy #81

Write an appreciation letter to your significant other. Expressing your appreciation can help prevent or minimize relationship complacency. After years of being in love, individuals have a tendency to take each for granted and fail to express their gratitude. A simple thank you can go a long way, especially if individuals are feeling unappreciated.

Write it here:

_____
_____
_____
_____
_____
_____
_____

Relationship Sustainment Strategy #82

Call your significant other at work at least once a week to inquire about his or her day. Demonstrate an interest in your significant other's professional life and offer support if he or she is stressed. You know him or her better than coworkers and can offer helpful coping information.

Write it here:

_____
_____
_____
_____
_____
_____
_____

Relationship Sustainment Strategy #83

Exhibit compassion and empathy toward your significant other. Compassion allows you to show mercy and remorse and is accomplished by placing yourself in your significant other's shoes. This allows you to be empathic. Trying to understand how your significant other feels will enable you to connect with him or her more effectively than focusing on their actions or words.

Write it here:

_____

_____

_____

_____

_____

_____

_____

Relationship Sustainment Strategy #84

Plan a date that you both will enjoy. This can be something you did when you first started dating or something completely new. Agree not to discuss stressful issues and spend the entire date reminiscing about the good times. Discuss joyful events and explore ways to relive them.

Write it here:

_____

_____

_____

_____

_____

_____

_____

-----------------------Unconditional Love-----------------------

Relationship Sustainment Strategy #85

Have a candle light dinner and hot bath with your significant other as often as time permits. Romance is healthy for the soul and spirit. Feelings of love are highest when individuals feel romantic or are being pampered. Make time to relax with your significant other.

Write it here:

_____
_____
_____
_____
_____
_____
_____
_____
_____

Relationship Sustainment Strategy #86

Write a letter of forgiveness if you are not good with words. Seeking forgiveness demonstrates feelings of remorsefulness and lets your significant other know that you care about his or her feelings.

Write it here:

_____
_____
_____
_____
_____
_____
_____
_____
_____

Relationship Sustainment Strategy #87

Practice paraphrasing and active listening to avoid misunderstandings and to clarify what you hear before responding. For example, "I heard you say……..and it makes you feel….."

Write it here:

_____
_____
_____
_____
_____
_____
_____
_____
_____

Relationship Sustainment Strategy #88

Do not listen to rebut. Pay attention to what is being said to you instead of thinking about your response. Process what your significant other is saying before you develop your response. This will allow you to get the real meaning of their message.

Write it here:

_____
_____
_____
_____
_____
_____
_____
_____
_____

------------------------Unconditional Love------------------------

Relationship Sustainment Strategy #89

Make a conscious effort to tell your significant other that you love him or her regularly. There may be days that your significant other needs to hear those words more than other days, so attempt to say them daily and with sincerity.

Write it here:

_____
_____
_____
_____
_____
_____
_____
_____
_____

Relationship Sustainment Strategy #90

Recognize that your participation is needed to make your relationship work. No relationship can survive if one person is doing all the work.

Write it here:

_____
_____
_____
_____
_____
_____
_____
_____
_____

Relationship Sustainment Strategy #91

Avoid power struggles. There is no room for "Me versus You" debates in healthy relationships. Competition causes individuals to demoralize others in order to gain an advantage. Emphasize "Us" and elicit "Win-Win" solutions.

Write it here:

_____
_____
_____
_____
_____
_____
_____
_____
_____

Relationship Sustainment Strategy #92

Praise your significant other publicly. Let family and friends know how wonderful your significant other is and talk big about his or her accomplishments.

Write it here:

_____
_____
_____
_____
_____
_____
_____
_____
_____

Relationship Sustainment Strategy #93

Focus on one issue at a time and do not bring up old issues. Bringing up old issues often complicates the issue at hand and it never gets resolved.

Write it here:

_____
_____
_____
_____
_____
_____
_____
_____
_____

Relationship Sustainment Strategy #94

Sweat the small stuff before it snowballs. If you are bothered by something, discuss it as opposed to suppressing it. Bottled up frustration will manifest itself in some form or fashion. Let your spouse know how you feel before you are consumed with resentment and anger.

Write it here:

_____
_____
_____
_____
_____
_____
_____
_____
_____

Relationship Sustainment Strategy #95

Set your significant other and relationship up for success. Expect only the best from him or her, but allow him or her to choose goals that are of value to him or her and give them the greatest satisfaction. Build up your significant other by focusing on and helping him or her capitalize on his or her God given internal drives and strengths.

Write it here:

_____
_____
_____
_____
_____
_____
_____
_____

Relationship Sustainment Strategy #96

Do not assign labels to your significant other. Labels such as lazy, inflexible and stubborn cause individuals to become defensive even if there is some truth to what is said. Simply describe the behavior without assigning a label to the person.

Write it here:

_____
_____
_____
_____
_____
_____
_____
_____

-----------------------Unconditional Love-----------------------

Relationship Sustainment Strategy #97

Discontinue habits that cause harm to your relationship: Gambling, excessive video game playing, partying, adult entertainment (strip clubs, porn movies, etc.), flirting, etc.

Write it here:

_____
_____
_____
_____
_____
_____
_____
_____

Relationship Sustainment Strategy #98

Encourage your significant other to express emotions when it is healthy and appropriate to do so. Emotions expressed in tense and unhealthy environments typically do not get resolved in a non-threatening or productive manner. There is a place and time for everything. Set the stage for healthy expression of emotions and coping.

Write it here:

_____
_____
_____
_____
_____
_____
_____
_____

Relationship Sustainment Strategy #99

Put God first in your relationship and the other 98 strategies can be accomplished effortlessly. To give and receive unconditional love you have to work. The good news is that most of the hard work and sacrifice has been done for you. Thank God!

Write it here:

_____

_____

_____

_____

_____

_____

_____

_____

_____

-----------------------Unconditional Love-----------------------

"Anything in life worth having is gained through diligence and work"

Are you prepared to work to sustain your relationship? Why or why not?

What can you do differently to sustain your relationship?

_____
_____
_____
_____
_____
_____
_____
_____
_____
_____
_____
_____
_____
_____
_____
_____
_____
_____
_____
_____

APPENDICES

Unconditional Love Stoppers

Appendix 1

Abusive Love Characteristics

As mentioned in chapter one, love does hurt, but not intentionally. To determine if you are in an abusive relationship review the characteristics below. If any of the characteristics are present in your relationship you should seek help immediately.

Types of Abuse

- Physical Abuse (inflicting physical discomfort, pain or injury) Slapping, hitting, burning, punching, restraining, sexually assaulting, handling roughly, etc.

- Sexual Abuse (forced sexual contact, rape or incest)

- Psychological/emotional abuse (diminishing your identity and self-worth) Threatening, insulting, name calling, yelling, imitating, ignoring, isolating, etc.

Physical Abuse

- Pushes or shoves you

- Physically restrains you to prevent you from leaving

- Slapped or bit you

- Kicks, chokes, hits or punches you

- Locks you out of the house

- Abandons you in a dangerous place

- Refuses to help you when you are sick or injured

- Subjects you to reckless driving

- Forces you off the road or keeps you from driving

- Rapes you

- Threatens or hurts you with a weapon

-----------------------Unconditional Love-----------------------

Sexual Abuse

- Makes demeaning remarks about you
- Insists that you dress in a more sexual provocative way than you desire
- Calls you derogatory sexual names like "whore" or "freak"
- Forces you to strip when you do not want to
- Forces you to have unwanted sex with others or forces you to watch others
- Forces sex after beatings
- Forces sex for the purpose of hurting you with objects or weapons
- Commits sadistic sexual acts

Emotional Abuse

- Puts you down
- Makes you feel bad about yourself
- Calles you names
- Makes you think you are crazy
- Plays minds games with you
- Humiliates you
- Makes you feel guilty

Dominate Actions

- Treats you like a servant
- Makes all the big decisions
- Acts like the "master of the castle"
- Defines roles and responsibilities

-----------------------Unconditional Love-----------------------

Economic Abuse

- Prevents you from working
- Controls the money and makes you ask for it
- Gives you an allowance
- Takes your money
- Restricts your access to family funds

Uses Bullying and Intimidation

- Makes or carries out threats to do something to hurt you
- Threatens to leave you or to commit suicide if you leave
- Makes you drop charges
- Forces you to do illegal things
- Uses threatening looks or gestures to frighten you and control you behavior
- Smashes household items
- Abuses the children
- Displays weapons

Using Children

- Makes you feel guilty about your interaction with the children
- Uses the children to control your actions
- Threatens to take the children away from you

Using Isolation

- Controls what you do, who you see and talk to, what you read and where you go

-----------------------Unconditional Love-----------------------

- Limits your outside involvement
- Uses jealousy to justify actions

Minimizing, Denying, Blaming

- Makes light of the abuse and does not take your concerns about it seriously
- Denies abusing you
- Accuses you of the abuse

Manipulative attempts to keep you in the relationship or get you back if you leave

- Treats you very well; apologizes, does whatever you ask
- Treats the children well
- Seeks help – attend counseling

Personality Make-Up of Abused Victims

- Has low self-esteem
- Has traditionalist views
- Blames self for perpetrator's behavior
- Suffers from guilt, yet denies terror and anger
- Has severe stress reactions with psycho physiological complaints
- Uses sex as a way to establish intimacy
- Believes that no one will be able to help her resolve her predicament

Personality Make-up of Perpetrators

- Has low self-esteem

------------------------Unconditional Love------------------------

- Believes all the myths about battering relationships
- Is a traditionalist
- Blames others for his actions
- Is pathologically jealous
- Presents a dual personality
- Has severe stress reactions
- Uses sex as an act of aggression
- Does not believe violent behavior should have negative consequences

Reaction of Victims

- Denial
- Blaming self
- Ambivalence

Long-Term Effects of Abusive Relationships

- Physical
- Mental
- Economic
- Children

Do you are your significant other possess any of the characteristics listed above? If yes, what is your plan to eliminate or change them? Write it here:

_____

_____

_____

_____

_____

-----------------------Unconditional Love-----------------------

Appendix 2

Abuse Screening Questionnaire

If you answer yes to one or more of the questions below, please talk to someone you trust and seek help.

Has your significant other touched you without your consent?

Has your significant other ever made you do things you didn't want to do?

Has your significant other taken anything that was yours without asking?

Has your significant other ever scolded or threatened you?

Are you afraid of your significant other?

Do you have low self-esteem because your significant other belittles you?

Do you feel like you are emotionally unstable in your relationship?

Do you often feel depressed, anxious or angry due to relational conflict?

Do you feel hopelessness, guilt or sadness due to relationship stress?

Are you overly compliant or passive in your relationship?

Are you extremely aggressive or demanding in your relationship?

Are you extremely dependent on your significant other?

Seek help immediately if you are being abused.

------------------------Unconditional Love------------------------

Appendix 3

Defense Mechanisms

How do you protect yourself from emotional harm? By physical means or by using defense mechanisms?

If you are incapable of protecting yourself physically, you are likely to rely on defense mechanisms. Defense mechanisms are psychological strategies that manifest to help individuals maintain a "healthy" self-esteem or image of self. Individuals commonly use defense mechanisms to defend themselves from dreadful and anxiety provoking thoughts, emotions and behavior. Defense mechanisms are not necessarily bad unless they are counterproductive to your emotional or physical well-being. Most individuals use defense mechanisms when they are unable to cope with a particular situation. Listed below are some of the common defense mechanisms that my clients have used.

1. **Rationalization** – providing a logical or intellectual explanation as opposed to the real reason

    a. I am to busy to be in a relationship, when the real reason is that you are afraid

2. **Intellectualization** – avoidance of unacceptable or uncomfortable emotions by focusing on the intellectual aspects

    a. Focusing on the details of the divorce or separation as opposed to the unhappiness and heartache caused by it.

3. **Projection** – placing unpleasant or unacceptable impulses within yourself onto others

--------------------Unconditional Love--------------------

194

a. If you are losing an argument with your significant other, you state "You are Stupid"

4. **Suppression** – pushing into the unconscious

   a. Trying to forget that your relationship is coming to an end or the pain associated with it

5. **Denial** – fighting against an anxiety provoking stimuli by stating it does not exist

   a. Denying that your significant other's report that he or she does not love you anymore is correct

6. **Displacement** – taking out your impulses out on a less threatening target

   a. Talking bad to your significant other in a cruel manner because you are mad with or upset at your boss

7. **Repression** – placing memories into the unconscious

   a. Forgetting about physical, emotional or sexual abuse due to the trauma and anxiety

8. **Regression** – returning to a previous developmental stage

   a. Leaving the house and slamming doors; screaming and pouting when your significant other does not do as you wish

As mentioned, defense mechanisms are not necessarily bad- how you express them determines if they will be counterproductive to you. It is important to be aware of defense mechanisms and learn effective coping skills to deal with the ones that cause distress and conflict in your relationship.

------------------------Unconditional Love------------------------

Scheduling For Seminars, Speaking Engagements or Film Screenings

Dr. Buckingham conducts seminars, speaking engagements and film screenings for groups, churches, and organizations throughout the year.

"Unconditional Love" is one of the most requested seminars; however, Dr. Buckingham conducts seminars and speaks on a variety of topics related to relationship difficulty, personal growth, stress management, effective leadership and team building.

RHCS is dedicated to expanding the horizons of all humans!

To book Dr. Buckingham for your next event:

R.E.A.L. Horizons Consulting Service, LLC
P.O. Box 2665
Silver Spring, MD 20915

240-242-4087 Voice Mail
www.realhorizonsdlb.com

I hope this book has been a blessing to you and I welcome your comments.
dwayne@realhorizonsdlb.com

--------------------Unconditional Love--------------------

This book can also be purchased on-line at:

www.realhorizonsdlb.com

Amazon.com

Target.com

BarnesandNoble.com

BooksaMillion.com

About the Author

Dwayne L. Buckingham, Ph.D., LCSW, BCD, is a psychotherapist and the Chief Executive Officer and Founder of R.E.A.L. Horizons Consulting Service, LLC in Silver Spring, Maryland. A commissioned officer in the United States Air Force, for nearly a decade he provided psycho-logical assessments and treatment to over ten thousand individuals, couples, groups, and families worldwide. Dr. Buckingham currently serves as a commissioned officer in the United States Public Health Service and provides individual and marital therapy to military troops assigned to the Walter Reed National Military Medical Center in Bethesda, Maryland. Dr. Buckingham is also an active member of the National Association of Social Workers and Kappa Alpha Psi Fraternity, Inc.

He is driven by the belief that every individual can improve his or her ability to cope with life challenges productively if given the opportunity and right support. Dr. Buckingham reminds individuals daily that a little understanding and education eliminates barriers and enables individuals to grow. He views his role as a community resiliency consultant. Through consultation and training, he hopes to provide individuals with the knowledge and skills essential to establishing and maintaining a positive and productive lifestyle.

Dr. Buckingham conducts seminars for groups, families, organizations, and churches each year. Please visit his website at www.realhorizonsdlb.com for more information.

www.ingramcontent.com/pod-product-compliance
Lightning Source LLC
Chambersburg PA
CBHW022358280326
41935CB00007B/228

9 780984 942329